Renegade M.D.

A DOCTOR'S STORIES FROM THE STREETS

Susan Partovi, M.D.

RENEGADE PRESS

Copyright 2023

ISBN: 978-1-66789-161-3 (print)
ISBN: 978-1-66789-162-0 (eBook)

TABLE OF CONTENTS

Introduction 1

1—Leprosy 7

2—To Stent or Not to Stent 14

3—Pedro 22

4—First Patient of the Day 32

5—Nec Fasc..49

6—Tragicare..56

7—Elbow Fracture; Big Dude...64

8—Free Will...66

9—Free Will, Part 2 76

10—The American Dream?...84

11—Daniel's Story...93

12—Cookie 107

13—Missing Paris 117

14—Treat, Don't Incarcerate 124

15—It's Not Okay with My Soul.................................... 128

16—New Kid; Good Doctor 135

17—Tina Marie 144

18—Sometimes Rock Bottom is Death 151

19—Tragedies and Triumphs 159

20—Mourning the Gentle Souls 166

21—Let's Keep the Gravely Disabled out of the Grave 172

22—Behind the Muddied Glass 177

23—Mental Illness, Meth, and Skid Row: Making it Happen . 186

24—I Know Death; Hope for Haiti 210

Excerpt from *This is Haiti* 213

INTRODUCTION

WHEN I STARTED TELLING STORIES TO MY COLLEAGUES ABOUT some of the patients I treated while working with PEH (people experiencing homelessness), one of my best friends suggested I write them down. So, I did. I also started responding to op-eds in the *Los Angeles Times* and writing letters to the editor about issues relating to the homeless. In 2007, I asked the then editor how to submit an op-ed of my own, and I submitted my story about William. When it was approved, I realized I had something to say, and people liked reading my stories. In the ensuing years, the situation for PEH hasn't changed much. There is more research proving the importance of supportive housing, and homelessness is given more attention by politicians and the media. But tens of thousands have been living on the streets of L.A. for decades. We have made some strides—more money appropriated, more outreach workers and street medicine teams, more interim housing—but the suffering is the same, especially for those struggling with severe mental illness.

Covid-19 gave those of us working with PEH an excuse to get more organized, and in some cases, more resources became available. Fortunately, Covid-19 didn't inflict its greatest assault on PEH unless they were in shelters. At the start of the pandemic, I sent an email to the handful of street practitioners I knew, suggesting we meet weekly to compare events and protocols. We started having regular, ongoing meetings that allowed us to learn from one another.

Because of Covid-19, we were able to use hotels to get more at-risk folk indoors. Brilliant! But the severely mentally ill were still in the streets, still eating out of garbage cans, filthy, yelling at hallucinations, getting incarcerated and released to the streets again and again. In recent years, owners of board and care facilities for the mentally ill are selling because they are not fairly reimbursed. For those who need advanced care and support, there are few such facilities. After PEH are hospitalized for mental illness, they are usually released back to the streets because there is nowhere for them to go! We need to focus on housing that heals, finding places for our most vulnerable so they're able to fully recover.

When I started practicing street medicine in 2007, I remember walking along the Santa Monica Promenade one morning. I grew up in Brentwood and Santa Monica, so this was my backyard. The "new mall" adjacent to the Promenade was built while I was in junior high school, and the Promenade itself while I attended college. It soon became the westside's weekend hangout for movies, shopping, and dining. That morning, it was sunny and quiet but busy with locals getting their breakfast or shopping in the swanky shops. Also, PEH were hanging around. I noticed an older woman, who looked to be in her eighties but probably was younger. Living on the streets ages people quickly. This woman didn't look unkempt, but she wore a long, flannel nightgown with pink flowers, and ratty slippers. She was asking for money.

"Hi," I said. "Do you need any medical help?"

She squinted in the bright sun. "Are you gonna give me money?"

"No."

"Then leave me alone!"

I thought of my grandmother, who had recently passed away in her nineties. She had been quite the matriarch of my dad's large, Persian-Jewish family. My father and his siblings took great care of Grandma and Grandpa. Grandma developed dementia after my dad passed, and she required round-the-clock care. If my grandmother had wanted to panhandle on the Promenade in her flannel nightgown, I would have picked up all four feet, nine inches of her, tucked her under my arm, and thrown her into my car. My aunts and uncles would have all done the same in a heartbeat.

I realized this cantankerous woman before me WAS someone's grandmother, mother, sister, or aunt. She might as well have been mine. I would never allow my family member to live on the streets (and had to face this possibility when both my mom and then, my sister, became incapacitated). Why do we, as a society, allow it? Americans like to think that here, we have free will. But why can't we recognize that some people lack the ability to make rational decisions for their well-being— like children, those with intellectual disabilities, and those who are demented? We recognize *their* inability. Why can't we give the same urgency of care to those with severe mental illness?

For my entire career as a doctor, I have strived to take a stand, so that all suffering from demons can be cared for—just like my own grandma, mom, and sister. I hope by reading these stories, you'll recognize the shared humanity of these most vulnerable members of our society and join me in my efforts to treat them like family.

For all my patients. May their voices be heard!

1

LEPROSY

"Leprosy!" my mentor, Steve, announced.

We stood next to each other in a five-by-ten-foot room with a cement floor, two walls of plywood shelves filled with various medications, and one bed behind a makeshift curtain made from an old, ratty sheet.

We stared down at the man's feet—a red, white, and greenish menagerie of flesh.

Steve called out for Anne, a surgical nurse. "Assist me, por favor." He straightened up and sweat gleamed from his high forehead. A thirty-year-old engineer who had trained as a physician's assistant, Steve was short, with a full moustache and a love of Christian music. We listened to his cassette tapes on our drives to and from Mexico.

"What do we have?" Anne, an industrious volunteer, poked her head in.

The patient was sitting on an upside-down bucket being used as a stool. Around sixty, he had a tan, leather face. On his lap sat a cowboy hat, which had left sweat-soaked hair plastered across his forehead.

"Debride!" Steve answered cheerfully.

It was 1986 and I was eighteen years old, in my first year at UCLA. I arrived with Steve and other volunteers. We had traveled in an old brown van, crossing the border where Mexican agents easily waved us through, past the large CaliMax market, then continuing toward downtown. Tijuana had a distinct smell, like grilled meat mixed with manure. Often, we'd pick up people along the narrow, bumpy road to the "clinic." In the sweltering heat of summer, packing what felt like an entire, sweaty village into the van annoyed me; later, I understood this was partially how the group served the community—by bringing them to church. That morning, we had arrived early at the squatter site, "el dumpay," our made-up Spanish name for "the dump." The clinic was literally on top of a hill above a valley of garbage.

Anne pushed aside the sheet-curtain and moved next to Steve. She seemed able to read his mind and would often start working on patients without direction.

I stepped aside, planting myself in a corner but close enough to observe. I was grossed out but excited at the same time. I didn't know anything about leprosy other than it was a skin disease discussed in the Bible. And here was Steve, helping a leper, just like Jesus. "How do you treat this?" I asked.

Steve explained the process of debriding, removing dead and infected skin. This, along with antibiotics, would allow the infection to heal. Then he asked Anne about dinner.

All day, patients would line up in the heat outside the clinic. They came for various reasons: diabetes, hypertension, infections. But the most coveted item was "Beeks," aka Vicks Vapo Rub. The windows of the clinic were covered with bars, and the patients yelled through them: "Doctor Esteeb, Beeks!"—the panacea for all that ailed them. They lived in shacks made from scraps of wood and fabric. They were the poorest of the poor and spent their days picking through the heaps of trash looking for recyclables or things for their homes—both adults and kids. I had heard there was an outhouse behind the church, which was behind the clinic, but after checking the facilities out, I had decided to try and hold it in all day.

Steve started cutting away sections of the man's infected feet. Anne handed him supplies and took away the pieces of tissue he handed back. My heart was pounding. A substantial chunk of the man's big toe came off and yet, they continued to review dinner choices—all part of this flowing, orchestral performance.

I felt completely engaged and alive. I had wanted to be a doctor since I was twelve years old. Finally, I was experiencing what I had been preparing for with all the science and math classes I'd taken. My way to science had been through math, with the assistance of people like Mrs. Gaspar, my third-grade teacher. I used to stay after class to help her clean up because my parents came home late from work. I loved Mrs. Gaspar. She was short and stumpy, with dark hair cut above her ears. We called her Mrs. Penguin because of the way she walked, but she always treated me with respect and like an adult, which I loved. When I asked why she had put me in Math 1, the remedial group, she said Math 2 was too crowded and she didn't want me to be overwhelmed in Math 3. Although I hadn't been a very confident kid and often worried about who liked me and who didn't, I was confident about school, and my abilities. I asked Mrs. Gaspar to let me try Math 3. She didn't question me or say, "What do you know? You're just a kid," like my mother would have.

My mother could be mean or degrading at times, competing with me for my dad's attention. As an adult, I can see we lacked that special, mother-child bond. I was closer to my dad, and though I knew he loved me, I didn't feel loved. He didn't tell me he loved me and wasn't very cuddly. And so, my entire life I chased love. *When will someone love me?* I persistently thought. Although Mrs. Gaspar wasn't lovey-dovey, she listened to me. I felt heard. In many ways, Mrs. Gaspar launched my scholastic career because she saw my ability and gave me a chance to prove myself. When Brentwood Elementary became a science magnet school, I discovered I liked science even more than math, and I was on my way.

I excelled in Math 3 and in school overall, which pleased my father. Being smart was common ground we shared because he had been a scholar, so to speak. Dad was born in Iran and had a master's degree in engineering, completed in the United States. When I mentioned the volunteer trip to Mexico, Dad had been suspicious of Steve at first. Eventually he acquiesced, but to be honest, I was my own person by then. I made my own decisions. No one helped me get into college, like parents do now. I picked my own classes, joined a sorority, chose my specialty, studied for the MCATs, and chose medical schools all on my own. From a young age, I was fairly capable and independent.

"Susan," Steve said. "Would you find us some more gauze, please?"

"And maybe some saline," Anne added.

"Sure." I edged around the patient's cot, never looking away from the bloody proceedings below his knees.

The clinic was disorganized, having been set up impromptu and run by a rotating crew of volunteers. As I rooted through the supplies kept on the shelves, I noticed a huge book, a 1984 edition of PDR (Physician's Desk Reference), which lists all medications and their uses (a highly valued source before the Internet!). I would remember that book, eventually studying it front to back to organize the supplies at hand into a system, and to educate myself about ways to best use what was available. But for now, I scanned the shelves for a box of gauze and a clear bottle of saline.

I had first traveled to the dumpsite in Tijuana in high school during an Easter break. A dozen teenagers and some college students had signed up through the Brentwood Presbyterian Church to build small houses for the locals. This was my first experience of poverty. I grew up on the Westside of Los Angeles. Up to that point, I didn't know about good neighborhoods or bad neighborhoods. I had never been downtown, or to east L.A., and definitely not to South Central.

Back in the makeshift exam room in Tijuana, I handed the medical supplies to Anne, who took them without taking her eyes off the now deformed foot. Steve was busy soaking up blood and reached for more gauze. I wasn't sure I had found enough.

"If you could wrap him," Steve said to Anne, handing her the final roll of gauze before he moved on to the next "room," the next patient.

In the 1980s, I had seen commercials with impoverished Ethiopians, but it didn't hit home until I saw it with my own eyes. But in Mexico I also discovered something about resilience. Amidst the trash and deplorable conditions, the children at the dumpsite still laughed and played. They raced around the clinic, waiting for their parents to be seen, or waiting to be seen themselves for conditions that mostly would have been considered routine in the United States. For them, minor health problems often persisted and caused much suffering. But still they played!

As I watched Anne gently wrap the man's feet, I remembered what a high school friend said to me, trying to convince me to join the trip to Tijuana. "Do something for someone else for once in your life." And she was right. I had been self-centered and often worried about how I looked or who liked me.

I started going to the clinic with Steve every Saturday, where I watched him use humor to put everyone at ease. I quickly began to learn Spanish, as I had taken French in high school, and I started to understand most of Steve's jokes. The patients loved him. I remember one Saturday we saw Hugo, who was a regular. He was in his forties, quite overweight and always very dirty. Due to poor circulation, his legs had venous stasis, which causes swelling and skin breakdown. This is common in diabetics and people with hypertension, and he certainly could have had both. Because of the poor circulation, he would get large ulcers, or wounds, on his legs, and he'd come in for treatment when things became unbearable. That Saturday, I carefully unwrapped the bandages he'd made with paper and a bandana. I blinked at what I saw underneath, almost not believing it. One of the wounds was teeming with maggots. By then, I had learned to not react to things that were gross. Hugo's eyes shifted away in embarrassment and at that same moment, Steve popped over to see what I was doing. He saw what was happening and without missing a beat, said, "Mm mm, lonche" (pronounced *lawn-chay*). Lunch!

We all burst out laughing, including Hugo, his wife, and several other patients lined up outside and watching through the barred window. Our laughter increased until some of us were in tears. From Steve, I learned the value of humor in making and keeping a connection with patients. As we finished and Hugo sat up, he gave a modest smile, although he'd been sweating throughout the procedure, often gripping the sides of the cot.

During my trips to Tijuana, these aspects of my identity up to that point—my love of science and desire to be a doctor, that first exposure to poverty by seeing the effects of famine on Ethiopian children, and maybe, a personal need to be appreciated and have a direction—all combined to crystallize into what would become my life's purpose, treating the impoverished. I made humor an important part of my bedside manner, and it felt good to bring laughter and ease to patients. If people living in poverty could still have a sense of humor and play, then why couldn't I? Besides, I easily related to patients. They seemed like regular folk to me, each patient a challenge to treat medically and communicate with effectively. I loved the challenges that showed up at the clinic in Mexico and later, in my own practice on the streets and in clinics and hospitals around Los Angeles. In my family, I sometimes felt unloved and unheard, but on top of a pile of garbage in another country, I loved and was loved back. Because of these early experiences in Mexico, I made the commitment to become a doctor and focus on patients who experience the worlds of poverty and injustice.

2

TO STENT OR NOT TO STENT

"PRONOUNCE HER," THE RESIDENT SAID. HE WAS TALL AND bright-eyed, a second-year resident—which meant he had one more year of experience than I did. Most of the time he was an asshole, arrogant and stand-offish. But now, his hands were shaking.

I was twenty-six years old, a family medicine intern rotating on the gynecology team at Harbor-UCLA Medical Center, a mid-size, public, teaching hospital in Torrance. Throughout my college years at UCLA, I continued traveling to Tijuana every Saturday, then left California for the first time to attend Thomas Jefferson Medical School in Philadelphia. But California was my home. I had chosen Harbor-UCLA, a county hospital, for my residency.

I looked at the resident, my "superior," then down at the hospital bed.

The patient, a forty-year-old woman from Guatemala who had come to the emergency room complaining of back pain and bloody vaginal discharge, had died. It was my first death as a doctor.

"Pronounce her."

At the time, I wasn't sure what that entailed. I put my stethoscope against the thin hospital gown and heard nothing. Her chest was completely still. I remember thinking how strange it was to place my stethoscope on someone and not hear the heart beating. To touch a body that wasn't moving.

I was about half-way through my internship. The long hours and lack of consistent sleep had messed with my mental state at times, but I loved being in the thick of chaos, the person in charge of making order. To this day, I still like the challenge of trying to figure out what's wrong with patients. And I like to think I'm a nice doctor, a compassionate doctor. Sometimes, even in my early years of doctoring, other physicians didn't understand my passion for doing the right thing.

For example, on my surgical rotation, every morning I checked on a young man who had an open wound due to infection. The chief resident, a confident, outspoken woman in her sixth year of training, would put on gloves and stick a finger inside the wound to check for tunnels, passageways formed underneath the skin that could lead to poor healing. The patient's face would scrunch up and he'd breathe rapidly throughout this procedure, obviously in much pain. I started arriving early, so I could order morphine and have it injected through his IV before the chief did her exam. She caught on and would wait for me to give him the medicine, but she'd also shake her head, scoffing at my desire to be gentle with him.

Another time, a patient's hemorrhagic pancreatitis was so bad, the entire abdomen left open to allow us to monitor and disinfect. My job was to clean the large wound with saline, and pack it with damp gauze to allow for healing. This process took an hour or so because we exchanged stories while I worked, and I took the time to listen when she asked to take a break. To alleviate her pain as much as possible, I proceeded slowly and gently.

There were many of these stories, many cases, many patients. Many opportunities to think about acting humanely and treating patients with dignity and respect. But this, my first death, this felt like a failure.

I stared at the woman before me, motionless and pale in the bed. She'd been with us for about a week. The first examining physician was a second-year gynecological resident. While I assisted and translated, he examined her, after insisting that her lower back was propped up on a cold, upside-down bed pan. He said it was easier for him that way, but it was painful for her.

After an initial exam, he announced without emotion, "Her cervix is rock hard."

When the patient looked at me for an explanation, I told her we'd take care of her and the pain. I told her she'd need a biopsy and tried to explain why. She was a petite, soft-spoken woman who'd never had a pap smear—a common scenario with people from less-developed countries. Later, a biopsy confirmed she had cancer, and a cat scan showed it had spread wildly and was blocking her ureters, the tubes that carry urine from the kidneys to the bladder. The cancer had also invaded her spine, which was the reason for her back pain. Her face was placid now, forever pain-free. Prior to the last couple of days, this woman exhibited a calm gentleness. She laughed easily, and her three children—teenagers and young adults—came to visit her daily. They surrounded her, telling stories and arranging things around the room: flowers, pictures, Guatemalan food.

One morning, shortly after she was admitted, a team including the chief resident, a small team of residents, and the attending physician, assembled at the nurses' station to discuss her case. As an intern, I felt a little lost. I didn't know much about advanced cancer, or end-of-life care. The attending and chief resident discussed whether to stent, or insert a tiny tube, into her ureters, to allow urine to flow through. If both ureters are blocked, the kidneys die. One can't live without working kidneys. *To stent or not to stent?* I felt like I was listening to a foreign language, catching every fourth word. "If we stent, she has a few more months to live—in pain. If we don't, she dies of kidney failure. All in all, it's not a bad way to die."

Apparently, dying of kidney failure is relatively painless. This is the conclusion I made at the time, and it was true. As the body's toxins slowly build up, the patient gets groggy, falls asleep and eventually, dies. That day, it was decided. Not to stent!

Wait! What?! Shouldn't we ask the patient? The family? Isn't there something we can do? I felt sick. I didn't know enough to say anything or ask the right questions aloud.

This decision had been made and yet, I didn't discuss it with the patient. Every morning, I saw her on my rounds, and I made sure her pain was well controlled. I avoided talking to her family because I didn't know what to tell them. We had made the decision without their input, and it felt wrong.

In those days, my moral compass was still being calibrated. As a kid, I often didn't know the right thing to do, as I hadn't received much guidance from my parents. My sister and I used to watch the television show *Little House on the Prairie,* which served, in many ways, as a moral teacher. Each episode dealt with some quandary, and the Ingalls family always came out on the right side, acting with kindness and respect for others. Right and wrong always seemed so clear on Little House. On the contrary, my mother would steal small things from stores or switch price tags. Once, she had me change the tag on a Donny Osmond cassette tape I asked to buy. I was around ten. As for my father, he had two sides. I was the apple of his eye, especially where my performance in school was concerned, but he was often angry. I think he was frustrated with his marriage. He later told me he had fallen out of love with my mom when I was an infant. His unhappiness in life resulted in a bad temper. Not like Pa on *Little House*! Pa rarely got angry, and if he did, it was for a good reason. Charles Ingalls filled my notions of what an ideal dad and husband should be like.

I continued to check on the cervical cancer patient from Guatemala, mostly to verify her pain relief. A couple of days after the decision not to stent, she started complaining of shortness of breath. This happens with acute kidney failure, when the kidneys aren't functioning and the fluid that's normally urinated seeps into the lungs. I found my chief resident near the nurses' station; the usual activity buzzed around her. I asked her what to do about the patient's breathing difficulty. The chief resident and I had never seen eye to eye. She was smart and seemed to know her stuff, but she could be short-tempered and always seemed annoyed by me. I wasn't sure if it was because I was a family physician—often looked down upon by some specialists—or because I was an intern, or because she didn't like it when I questioned her decisions.

"Lasix," she instructed.

She seemed impatient, as if she couldn't be bothered by me or the issue. Lasix is a medication that works on the kidneys to increase urine production and is a helpful solution when one has extra fluid in the body. But this patient's kidneys weren't working. I didn't think Lasix would work to rid her of the extra fluid spilling into her lungs.

I looked at the second-year resident, who, despite having a year more experience than I did, looked just as clueless. I looked back at the chief resident, not knowing what to say. At the time, I wasn't experienced with end-of-life care. I followed instructions and gave the patient Lasix and oxygen, hoping it would help her breathe easier.

Later that morning, I walked by her room. It was like watching a movie in slow motion. The scene replays itself in my mind, over and over, even now, after many years. As I passed by, hurrying to whatever it was I had to do, she was sitting on the edge of her bed, holding her head up high, trying to find the best position to breathe. It's called tripoding, and it's a sign of someone in desperate respiratory distress. I glanced into her room and kept walking. I didn't know what to do. I knew she was suffering. I kept walking.

An hour later, the nurse called to say the patient had expired. The second-year resident and I went into her room. She was lying still in the bed, her limbs in awkward positions. Her twenty-something-year-old daughter, who was always smiling when I saw her, was crying hysterically. She looked at me in desperation, as though begging me not to say the words.

"Pronounce her."

My heart was beating rapidly. I shook my head and said, "Lo siento." *I'm sorry.*

The daughter immediately started to hyperventilate, and her eyes rolled up. I rushed to her, pushing her head between her knees. As she wept, I held her, repeating, "Lo siento, lo siento." I looked up at the resident and we met eyes. I knew something was wrong, that we had done something wrong. At the time, I couldn't articulate *how* the patient's treatment had been wrongly handled, I just knew that it had been.

Death is tricky. It rarely goes well. That slow-motion reel as I passed the woman's room while she fought for air often haunts me. I should have comforted her better, explained what was happening, and reassured her relatives. As a family physician, I had learned the importance of full communication, which included immediate family. In fact, we often have family meetings when a patient is hospitalized. I wondered if gynecologists learned this, or if other specialists considered the support system for the patient. Shouldn't all doctors have the family in mind if they genuinely cared? Neither the attending nor the chief resident seemed to care. They didn't see this patient as an individual—with feelings, concerns, and family. So, why had they chosen medicine? For the surgery aspect? Something else?

Many years into my own practice, I realize now it's not a matter of whether you're a general practitioner or some type of specialist. I know plenty of Ob/GYNs and surgeons who care. Each doctor has an individual responsibility to care. When a collective of caring individuals—physician, church group, family, friends—comes together for a patient, we make better decisions. If our culture could prioritize "we" over "me," people would act collaboratively. Can I, as a doctor, teach people to care? Can I inspire, or say something to make a difference?

These questions began to bounce around in my head after that first painful loss of a patient. From that moment, I decided to fight for my patients, fight for their dignity and rights. My own moral compass was still under development after some conflicting examples from my childhood and my early experiences as a doctor. But I knew I would strive to treat my patients and all people as I'd want to be treated—with compassion, concern, and conscientiousness.

In high school, I started attending Bible study at a Presbyterian church in Brentwood, and my first trip to Mexico was with a church youth group on mission. When I told my family I'd become a born-again Christian, it was shock to some. My grandmother said in her broken English, "It's okay, God still loves you." For me, the appeal had mostly to do with Jesus and the principles he represented: empathy, love, and being of service to others less fortunate. After medical school, I stopped calling myself a Christian because of intolerances I saw in other Christians, but the basic ideas have stayed with me.

At Harbor-UCLA, I also began to develop a broader understanding of social justice (and injustice) issues that affect medical care. At this hospital that served many of the underserved in Los Angeles County, I was surrounded by similar-minded, passionate doctors who wanted to make a local and global difference. And it was there that my love for teaching grew. After my training, I stayed on for six more years as faculty and since then, teaching medical students has always been a part of my life. Role models are important. They were for me, and if we want to make changes on a broad level, we need to train future doctors about caring—the first requirement in treating any person.

3

PEDRO

PEDRO'S WIFE WAS MY PATIENT. I HAD JUST COMPLETED MY residency and was now a chief resident at Harbor-UCLA Medical Center. At the time, our Family Medicine Clinic was across the street from the hospital and campus. Mostly, we saw patients without medical insurance. Before the 2014 expansion of Medicaid, the uninsured had limited options but could receive care at a county hospital, and Harbor was one of the four county hospitals in Los Angeles. Pedro's wife came into the clinic regularly for hypertension. She was a sweet, Latina woman in her fifties, sassy and funny. One day as I examined her, she told me her husband was having stomach pains and difficulty swallowing. I told her to make an appointment for him.

The following week, they came in. Pedro was thin and angular, with thinning, whitish gray hair combed straight back from his forehead. When I asked about his stomach issues, he didn't seem overly concerned. I could tell he had come to please his wife, as he looked over at her often. He had a gentle and calm demeanor. I could tell he had lost weight due to his hollow cheeks. He confirmed that he had some difficulty swallowing food, and I was immediately concerned about cancer.

I ordered a Barium Swallow Study, which confirmed that he had an esophageal mass, most likely cancer. Someone at the clinic received the report before I saw Pedro again and made an urgent referral to surgery. The patient was whisked off to the land of surgeons, and I never had the chance to tell him in person about his diagnosis.

I didn't see him again until a couple of months later, when I ran into him strolling through the Harbor-UCLA hospital arm-in-arm with his wife. He was there for a post-op check-up, and he was holding a bag of popcorn.

"How did it go?" I asked.

"Great!" he exclaimed. "I can eat anything now!"

I smiled back at him, adopting his sense of ease and relief. I had to admit, he did look better. His face was relaxed, and he'd gained some weight. But I knew esophageal cancer was almost always terminal. I reminded him to make an appointment with me, and he said he would. I watched as they continued down the hall.

In the fifth grade, our teacher had brought in two sets of plastic-encased, preserved lungs. One was a healthy lung, Mr. Sawtelle told us, and one was from someone who had smoked for a long time. The healthy lung was pink, but the other was pale, with black flecks throughout. After school, I ran home to tell my dad about what I had seen and to forbid him from smoking another cigarette. Eventually, he quit. But twenty years later, he was struck with lung cancer.

I was in medical school when he told me, over the phone. He said it was small cell lung cancer, and he felt that God was punishing him. I didn't know how to respond, because we had never talked about God or feelings, in general.

No, I didn't talk about feelings with my father. Never had. I ignored his comment about his cancer being some sort of punishment and focused on the clinical questions. What kind? Had it metastasized? What was the treatment plan? When would it start? After we hung up, I researched everything. Small cell was an aggressive cancer, with low survival rates at five years. I chose not to dwell on that, blocking it out of my mind as I focused on his treatments.

My dad had always looked like the Shah of Iran, with olive skin, big brown eyes, and dark, bushy eyebrows. When he underwent chemotherapy, he lost all his hair, even his eyebrows. He didn't look like himself, but for a while, he was cured. A year later, the cancer returned.

I saw Pedro's wife a few weeks after seeing them at the hospital. She came to the clinic for a regular visit, and her blood pressure wasn't bad, considering what the family was going through. Pedro had an appointment with me the following week. At one point she lowered her voice and said to me very seriously, "By the way, don't tell Pedro his stomach was removed."

I looked at her. "Only sections of his esophagus and stomach were removed."

She nodded. "It's okay to say they removed part of his esophagus but not the stomach."

I'd never had a request like hers before and didn't know what to say.

"Why?" I asked.

Her eyes bore into mine. "He'll lose his will to live if he knows his stomach was removed. He thinks he had surgery to remove the obstruction."

"Did anyone tell him that he had cancer?"

She crossed her arms over her chest.

"No, and I don't want him to know."

In medical school, we'd learned that doctors should not be paternalistic or make decisions for their patients. My personal school of thought when it came to patient matters was to stick with full disclosure. I believed in fully informing the patient about their condition, prognosis, and possible treatments. This allowed them to make plans and decisions, say goodbyes, if necessary, get things in order, and guide their end-of-life care through advance directives. Patients need to answer questions like, "Do you want CPR if your heart stops?" and "Who do you want making medical decisions for you?"

The woman sitting across from me had set her face with unmovable determination. I didn't argue with her.

"He'll lose his will to live if he knows he has cancer," she said again. "And then, he will die sooner."

To her, death should be avoided at all costs and for as long as possible.

Before Pedro and his wife arrived for his next appointment, I asked Dr. Castro, one of our attending physicians, for advice. Dr. Castro was a charismatic, macho-looking doctor with a sleek moustache and a full head of shiny hair that he kept gelled stiff. In our department, we all knew him as someone who could most often make patients cry. He was compassionate, but a straight talker. He was also very smart, and he was my favorite attending physician. Although I was a chief resident, Dr. Castro had much more experience than I did, and I needed help.

I found him in the doctor's charting room and filled him in on the details about Pedro. I asked what I should do.

He looked up from the chart I had handed him. "About what?"

"The family doesn't want me to tell Pedro he has cancer, or that he doesn't have much time," I explained.

He nodded and handed me the chart. "Well, we need to understand what death means to this family. What is its purpose? What does their culture say about death? How do they interpret death and dying?"

Before he finished, tears were rolling down my cheeks. My dad had passed away two months earlier. I had learned that Persians also treated death as the enemy—not as a natural part of life, or a time to find peace. Death was an evil to fight tooth and nail, and accepting it was the betrayal of hope. "Miracles happen all the time," my family would insist as they held vigil over my father day and night.

When my dad's cancer returned, I was a third-year resident, living in Redondo Beach. He started a different chemotherapy protocol, lost his hair again. But this time, the treatment didn't work. The cancer persisted and continued to spread. Around this time, I went to Palm Springs with my dad and stepmom. My parents divorced when I was nineteen. He had dated a string of American-born women before meeting Fereshteh. During that trip to the desert, my dad refused to let either of us drive, and all he did was sleep once we reached the hotel. He never came to the pool, never walked with us around town. This was the first time I realized he wasn't really getting better, but my stepmom wouldn't discuss it.

Pedro's family also wanted to believe that he was "just" sick and would get better. As a physician, I knew the truth: he was dying. How could I help Pedro's family figure out what death meant when I didn't know myself? What was the purpose? I didn't know! What did it mean? I didn't know.

Ignoring my tears, Dr. Castro calmly walked with me to Pedro's room. Pedro and his wife were both there. He looked gaunter and his clothes were loose again, but he still had a spark in his eye.

Dr. Castro asked, "Do you want to know the details of your illness? For instance, if you were dying or had cancer, would you want to know?"

Without missing a beat, Pedro said, "No." And then he closed his eyes.

The clouds had lifted. What had seemed so complex became so simple.

For several months, Pedro continued to come to the clinic for checkups. I didn't tell him he had cancer, but I always searched his eyes, hoping to see if he had caught on. He remained blissfully and purposefully ignorant. It was settled. I, too, became comfortable in their world of denial—never thinking about what I would do when Pedro came closer to the end of his life.

One day, I visited my dad in his Malibu home. He opened the door wearing the green sweat suit I had bought him for Christmas (we were Jewish but celebrated the holiday). His clothes seemed bigger than I had remembered. We walked into the dark living room and sat down. He started talking about the house and whether he should pay it off before "you know." His eyes bore into mine. My stepmother, who had been standing nearby, left the room. He couldn't talk about his illness or impending death without upsetting her. She wouldn't hear anything about it and refused to be part of the discussion. She chose to believe he was going to get better.

In the kitchen, she kept a tin can for miracles. The can came from my cousin's synagogue and every time you passed by it, you were supposed to put in a penny for miracles. That's what it said, right on the can! My stepmom emptied her change into it regularly.

We went through his finances, and I told my dad the house shouldn't be paid off, and I gave him my opinions on certain topics.

Months after our first meeting, Pedro and his wife rushed to the clinic one day because he was having trouble breathing. He was obviously in distress. I quickly evaluated him and asked Dr. Castro what I should do, reminding him of our secret. Outside the room, he asked Pedro's wife discreetly, "Do you want everything done to keep him alive?"

Her face transformed into a look of pure panic. "Of course! And don't forget your promise. You heard him. He doesn't want to know anything."

I was confused. *He's dying! Let him go in peace!* We called 911 to have the paramedics take him to our emergency room across the street.

I ran over to update the ER docs about his case. They had put him in Bed #1, reserved for the sickest patients. His portable chest x-ray was on the view box behind his bed. His lungs were completely "whited out."

"Lymphangitic spread," the ER attending physician told me. The cancer had spread through the lymphatic system. His lungs were filled with fluid, which was causing his breathing difficulty.

I went to Pedro's bedside.

He was sitting upright, fighting for breath. His desperate eyes found mine. "Dr. Partovi, what's happening to me?" he asked breathlessly in Spanish. I remembered the cheerful woman from Guatemala, the first patient I had witnessed struggling for breath.

I caressed Pedro's head, smoothing back his hair while deciding what to say.

In typical Persian fashion, my uncle Jamshid decided to get married with only a few days' notice. Jamshid was the youngest of six children, and my father was the oldest, but they were best friends despite the fifteen-year age difference between them. My dad was getting sicker, and I think my uncle had moved up the ceremony so his brother could attend.

My dad and stepmom showed up at Jamshid's condominium, where the wedding was held. My father was swimming in his suit, and his face was severely emaciated. I watched him throughout the day. I could tell he was trying to follow what was happening, but at times, he looked confused. His once-beautiful eyes bulged out. But he didn't want to worry his beloved brother. Their parents, my grandparents, were there, but as I watched them during the celebration, I realized no one had told them he was sick.

The day after the wedding, my stepmom called to tell me that my dad was acting strangely. He couldn't walk or talk. She took him to the hospital, where they determined he'd had a stroke. He was discharged with the recommendation for a home hospice consultation. I drove up to see him as soon as I was done with patients.

He was lying in bed, unable to move. He looked so small in the middle of his king-sized bed. As I stood over him, I could tell he recognized me, and I could tell that he knew he was dying. He couldn't speak. I sat on the bed and leaned over. Sections of my long curly hair fell across my face. Reaching up, he touched a few strands.

"Yes, it's long," I said. "You never did like my hair long."

He looked away. I felt horrible. His last attempt at communicating with me was a demonstration of love, touching my hair gently, and I had slapped it away with my words. We had often been at odds with each other. With both parents, I was always trying to prove that my opinion mattered. When I was a child, he cut my hair himself. He'd say, "Curly hair has to be short, period!" Finally, they allowed me to go to a salon, but my mom told the hairdresser to cut it short, at my father's insistence. I was in the fifth grade, and the kids at school laughed when I showed up the next day looking like Liza Minelli. After that, I never let either of them touch my hair. I grew it down to my waist.

I looked at Pedro, determined to be straightforward with him, somehow. "Your lungs are filled with fluid," I said. "We're giving you medicine to help you breathe." The attending physician had left, and we were alone at that moment. I wanted to tell him he was dying, but I kept my promise to his family, and to him. Later that week, he died in the hospital. At every moment, he was surrounded by multiple family members, who would remind the team taking care of him to keep Pedro in the dark about his cancer, and his condition. No one ever told him.

My dad died three weeks after his brother's wedding. At first, my stepmom didn't want to sign the Do Not Resuscitate forms required by the home hospice service. She kept insisting on her potential miracle. My cousin and I, both doctors, searched through my dad's things and finally found paperwork confirming he did not want life-sustaining treatment in the case of a terminal illness. Finally, she signed. Hospice brought a hospital bed and a wheelchair. Eventually, I hired round-the-clock help when it became too much for my stepmom to handle.

I felt like a zombie for the first, few months after my father's death. I graduated residency feeling like a zombie, carried out my chief resident duties often feeling like a zombie As a doctor, we learn the patient is first priority. But I came to realize how important it is to care for the family, too. They are the ones who deal with the aftermath, second guessing every course of treatment and every conversation with their loved one. *Did we do everything we could have?* My grandmother was in her nineties when my father died, and the light inside this bright and witty woman dimmed substantially. She was never the same; in many ways, she gave up. As a doctor, we see patients who come from a variety of circumstances and cultures. Some can't afford the type of care we were fortunate to have for my dad. Some families face a terminal diagnosis head on; others choose to bury their heads in the sand. Learning to listen to what is best for your patient—for them, *and their family*—is something I learned from Pedro's wife and family, and from Pedro himself. A good doctor guides her patients and doesn't project her own sense of right and wrong onto them. It's the family who will continue thinking about their lost loved one long after the doctor leaves the scene.

4

FIRST PATIENT OF THE DAY

Bob, an eager medical assistant at the Venice Family Clinic, told me about my first patient. "This is a sweet, old man with diabetes who hasn't been here for six years. I remember him because he had a huge boil on the back of his neck, and he'd come in for daily packing. He was hospitalized for three months because of that boil!"

I had started working at several clinics around L.A. and saw patients regularly at the homeless winter shelters. I attended national conferences on homeless medicine, participated in committees dedicated to improving medical care in vulnerable communities, and often gave presentations and lectures on several topics.

I looked at Bob, already anticipating his answer to my question. "Where has he been going for care since?"

He shrugged. "Nowhere. His brother brought him today. Says he's been living with him and his wife."

Great. He'd probably had every complication of diabetes by now. I scanned the chart quickly as I entered the room. "Antonio?"

He looked up, and my first impression was that he seemed child-like, even with a white, freshly trimmed beard. There was one spot he had missed under his neck, and this section of hair stuck out, like when a toddler tries to trim his own hair.

"Yes," he said. His face was wrinkled, but innocent and calm. This, along with the way he sat upright, swinging his legs over the side of the bed, completed my initial impressions of a childish demeanor. He wore a collared shirt, slacks, white socks, and sandals. The right sock was stained brown over the big toe—with dried blood.

I stepped closer and noticed a smell like mothballs. Another man, similar in age but a bit younger, stood in the corner of the room. The men looked alike. I assumed this was the brother and nodded at him before turning to the patient. "What brings you in today, Antonio?"

"My foot," he said. "It hurts something terrible! Can you give me a pain pill?"

I nodded. "I can give you something for pain. But first, are you taking any medications presently?"

Antonio and the brother simultaneously replied, "No."

I made a note on the chart. "Do you take medicines for your diabetes?"

He crossed his arms over his chest. "No, they didn't work for me."

"When was the last time you took diabetes medicine?"

He looked at me, his eyebrows creasing together. "Maybe it was Sunday?"

The brother took a step forward. "About five years ago."

"When was the last time you saw a doctor?"

Antonio shrugged, looking nervous now as he watched his sibling.

"Also, five years ago," the brother said.

I glanced at him, and his face was tense with exasperation. I looked back at Antonio, who lifted the foot with the stained sock.

"I have an ingrown toenail," he said. "Can you take off the nail?"

He wanted to get to the point and seemed to believe this was the cure.

"Well, let's take a look." I helped him remove his sandal and peel back the sock.

Hm, not quite an ingrown toenail. It may have started as such but now, his big toe was a volcano of exploding colors. The top was covered with a thick black crust, like dried putty. This was dry gangrene, dead tissue after the blood supply has been cut off. A large black and purplish blister extended from the cuticle over the entire distal, or lower, toe. This was wet gangrene, which occurs when bacteria invade dead tissue and cause infection. The rest of the toe was a bright pink, berry color. This was cellulitis, another type of skin infection. Dry gangrene covered a section of his middle toe as well. His overgrown toenails looked like claws, curving toward the big toe as if pointing to their sick member.

"So, can you take off the nail?" Antonio looked at me wide-eyed, ready for his cure.

"You need to be hospitalized," I said. "You'll need antibiotics and surgery." I didn't use the word *amputation.*

He thought about that for a moment. "Can you do it here?"

"No." I patted his knee. "They'll take good care of you at the hospital. They have good pain medicine."

Later, as the brothers sat in the waiting room, I updated Antonio's chart in the charting room. My thoughts swirled. Developmentally delayed or demented, Antonio was clearly unable to take care of himself. It was unacceptable that he hadn't seen a doctor for over five years—this was definitely neglect, maybe elder abuse. I resolved to report him to the Adult Protective Services (APS). On the form, this would require "Neglect" checked off as a type of abuse. I tried to convince myself that he needed placement in a suitable facility. He couldn't take care of himself, and his brother wasn't providing care.

Finally, I made up my mind. "Neglect" checked, phone call made to the APS, form faxed, ER referral filled out. But as I went about the rest of my day, interrupting a sense of "job well done" was a little voice that made me doubt my actions. I continued to ruminate about it. In the very least, he'd had a place to stay—which is more than some. If he didn't have his brother, he would have been homeless, smelling worse than mothballs, and wearing a much longer beard. That "Neglect" box on the form lingered in my mind.

Antonio was clearly neglected, but maybe there were gradations of neglect? People experiencing homelessness (PEH) and mentally ill were often neglected—by themselves, their families, and the city, county, state, and country. On an elder abuse form, I could check a box to accuse a conservator of neglect, but how did I report the thousands of neglected PEH who couldn't take care of themselves?

What about the man who sat on the Boardwalk in Santa Monica near the public restrooms between Stations 26 and 27? He kept his prized possessions in a shopping cart. Like many PEH, his skin was over-bronzed from constant sun exposure, and he hadn't showered for a long time. Weekly, I rollerbladed by, noticing his huge, swollen legs and shoeless feet. *Heart Failure? Kidney Failure? Liver Failure?* I pondered the causes of his leg swelling as I whizzed by. Who was responsible for his neglect? The city of Santa Monica? Los Angeles County? California? The U.S.? What form could I fill out to report this abuse?

About ten years later, my sister started to show signs of abnormal behavior and dementia. Eventually, she was diagnosed with a deteriorating neurological disorder, Frontal Temporal Lobe Dementia, which affects behavior, memory and speech. Later, my experiences trying to advocate and care for her made me rethink Antonio's situation.

The one thing I remember about my sister—before she became ill—was her laugh. Really, she was a giggler. It was a high-pitched, nervous sort of laugh, but she giggled at everything. Once when we were young, my dad was yelling at us about something, and she couldn't stop laughing. This made me laugh, which made my dad even more upset, which made us laugh even more. She was funny, too. Even as her memory was deteriorating and her caretaker had convinced her to cut her matted hair, she said in her wise-cracking way, "Great, now I look like a boy." She'd had beautiful hair—dark, curly, and down to her shoulders. She always wore make-up and earrings, calling herself a "princess."

Michelle was a high school French teacher at Lancaster High School. We had different dads, and her father and stepmother were French. During her twenties, she spent several years in France working as a nanny. She loved being a teacher because she loved her students. She went above and beyond for the kids. Once, she helped an eighteen-year-old student escape an abusive parent, and she helped another with her college application and tuition. After she'd been let go, one of her students sent me a message on Facebook, saying Michelle had been his favorite teacher in high school. He said she would play games to help them learn and create projects to keep the students entertained for two-hour blocks.

After coming out in her twenties, Michelle had a huge blow-out with my mom. She moved away and isolated herself from both of us. She didn't realize that I'd also been experiencing a period of disconnect from our mother. In 2008, Michelle reached out to me on Facebook. I drove up to Lancaster to see her and meet her partner. It was like we'd never been apart. Michelle had worried that I'd be uncomfortable with her lesbianism because I had become a Christian in high school. It broke my heart to think that my religion had potentially kept us apart. I really liked Sue, her partner. Soon after I reunited with Michelle, she started visiting our mom, who at that time was in the beginning phases of dementia. Sue went along; she had a lot of patience and enjoyed talking to my mom. For a couple of years, everything was going well.

In 2010, Sue died in a car accident. Immediately afterward, I spent some time with my sister and even helped teach her French class one day. Her students brought flowers and cards, and her friends were kind and supportive. We had a lovely memorial service, and I went with Michelle to see her partner's body. The woman who had lovingly prepared the body suggested Michelle not view it. She mentioned a dragon tattoo, and Michelle nodded, as she knew that tattoo well. My sister seemed to appropriately grieve Sue's death; she even went to therapy for a while. We talked regularly and saw each other a few times a year. But a couple of years after Sue's death, Michelle's father passed away. She had lived with him most of her childhood, not with our mother, and they were quite close. I'm not sure if these traumas contributed to or accelerated her problems.

The last time I remember a "normal" encounter with my sister was in 2012. She came to meet me at my clinic in Hollywood, and we went out to dinner and saw the Broadway show, *Wicked*. During dinner, she gave me a donation check for my non-profit, which sends medical students to work in Haiti. I was touched, especially because she was living on a teacher's salary. In the next few years, every time I spoke with her on the phone, she would say the same things, like a recording. "I'm eating healthy and not gaining weight," "The administration at my school sucks," and chit-chat about her pets. It was always the same, basic conversation.

When returning from a trip to Mammoth in 2014, I stopped by her house. This was a common scenario; I often went to the mountains and would swing by on the way to say hello. But that time, her house was a disaster. She had always been very neat. She seemed a little embarrassed and acknowledged she needed to do some cleaning but didn't say much else about it. In the summer of 2015, Michelle drove down to visit, and she seemed manic and said inappropriate things. She wasn't herself. When we went to dinner, she looked up from the menu and asked, "What do I like?"

A month after that, a coworker at the high school called me. "Michelle was walked off the campus," she said. "Something's wrong." I drove up that weekend, and her house was even worse. She had two dogs and two cats, and there was poop everywhere. Her mail, debris, her belongings—everything was all over the place.

The next weekend, my housekeeper and I cleaned up. I went through every piece of mail, including the letters from her work, and found a paper trail. Michelle hadn't been teaching; mostly, she'd show movies during class time. Students and parents had been complaining. She'd been calling in sick too often and once, she had shown up to work in her pajamas. I shook my head as I read. Why hadn't anyone called her next of kin to report this? Did they think she was just being lazy, or acting out?

As a physician, I know psychotic diseases don't start at age fifty-two. Michelle's memory was slipping. Was she depressed? She had lots of reasons—loss, childhood trauma. Sometimes, severe depression can include bizarre behavior and memory issues. But she didn't seem depressed. She was hyped-up and obsessive. She wouldn't let the dogs out in the backyard, worried that crows would eat them. She stressed about money. Constantly, she asked people to take her to the bank or an ATM. I called Michelle's primary doctor and asked for an appointment. I thought they could assess and possibly refer her to psychiatry. When we spoke, her doctor mentioned that the year before, Michelle had refused hospitalization when she'd had pneumonia. The doctor had sent a social worker to check on her, and they'd reported that everything was okay. I couldn't believe the social worker had been thorough. Had they seen the mess inside Michelle's home? Although my sister had seen medical professionals, they didn't think anything was wrong. Or maybe no one wanted to bother with the warning signs that must have been there.

Eventually, Michelle received her notice of termination from work. She was worried about money. I told her we could apply for disability, so she'd have a steady income.

"It's only two thousand a month," she told me, sounding somewhat reasonable. "I can't live on that."

"Maybe you can work as a tutor," I remember saying. At the time, I didn't fully understand her prognosis.

She met with the school's human resources department, and I had asked one of her friends to go along, in the hopes that Michelle wouldn't cash out her benefits. But she did. Now, she had some money in the bank. I thought she'd stop worrying and get better.

She didn't. When we talked on the phone, it was the same routine.

I'd ask if she'd found a job yet, and she'd say no. She'd tell me about her pets, and that she was eating healthy food.

Then I received another call from a neighbor. "Michelle looks really bad. She's wandering the streets, knocking on doors asking for money." The next week, she called to tell me Michelle had put antifreeze in her oil tank and now, her car wasn't running. She kept asking for rides to the market.

At that point, I hadn't seen my sister in over a year. I drove up to her place, and she was waiting for me in the driveway. It was winter and raining. She was wearing a purple jacket and holding an umbrella. Her hair was in a matted bun. She had lost about fifty pounds, and her face was leathery. But it was her teeth I'll never forget. Stained and obtrusive, they seemed too big for her face.

She got in the car, and I said, "We're going to the doctor for a check-up." On the way to the ER, I thought about what to say to get their attention: *altered mental status and failure to thrive.* Michelle had lost her Kaiser insurance when she lost her job, so I took her to the Antelope Valley Hospital Emergency room.

She kept asking the same questions over and over. "Why are we here? Can we go? I'm hungry." Her lab tests were normal, but the CT scan showed some temporal atrophy in her brain. I still hadn't connected this to her final diagnosis. I remember telling the genuinely nice ER doctor, "She used to look like me." Meaning, she didn't used to look like a psychotic, homeless woman.

We left the hospital and stopped at the market before I took her home. Her diet had completely changed. Mostly, she was eating bagel bites and popcorn. Back at her place, I met her sweet and caring neighbor. She told me Michelle would come over six times a day, asking for a ride to the market. Then, she would give her food away. I immediately called a mobile notary and had Michelle sign a power of attorney form, allowing me to make business and healthcare decisions for her. I didn't know what was wrong, but something was wrong. Taking care of my mom with Alzheimer's had taught me that getting POA papers was key. In actuality, the whole situation was way too familiar, but I tried not to think about it and focus on what needed to be done.

I called a friend of mine in neurology. After explaining Michelle's condition, he said it could be FTD, frontal temporal lobe dementia. This occurs when there is atrophy of the frontal lobe (which controls behavior and impulse) and the temporal lobe (which controls memory and speech).

It made sense. He also told me that FTD patients crave carbohydrates, and that clicked. I researched FTD, and everything he said aligned. It's a genetic disease that causes deterioration of the frontal and temporal lobes. The life expectancy is ten years after onset of symptoms. It used to be called Pick's disease. A light bulb went off. I had studied Pick's disease in medical school, and I remember thinking it was the worst disease anyone could get, because of the early onset and rapid personality change.

In the ensuing weeks, I hired someone to visit Michelle twice a week to make sure she had enough food and was eating. I took her to DPSS (Department of Public Social Services) to apply for Medi-Cal and Food Stamps (thank God for expanded Medicaid!). The caretaker made appointments for her with a primary care provider, a neurologist, and psychiatrist at the local county clinic. We needed to control her behavior, as the neighbors were still getting daily visits. She had started walking into backyards and houses—when she found an unlocked door. Soon, I hired more help and was able to get IHSS (In Home Supportive Services) for her, because MediCal paid for in-home care. I signed her up for SSI (Supplemental Security Income), getting help from a legal colleague who worked with Public Counsel. We were denied SSI, but due to her severe disability, she was approved for Medi-Care.

After a few months, it became clear Michelle needed round-the-clock care. She wouldn't take her medications on her own and eventually, would become a danger to herself. Later that year, I moved her and her pets in with my mom, who already had 24/7 caretakers. I offered to pay more, of course, and prepared the spare room. My mom was on board. She didn't really understand what was going on, but when I asked if Michelle could move in, she said yes.

Michelle's behavior was becoming increasingly erratic and difficult. She wandered a lot, bothered my mom, and didn't sleep well. I knew that eventually, I needed to find another place for her. I brought her to the FTD (frontotemporal dementia) specialist at UCLA, who confirmed her disease but couldn't offer advice or help. There isn't much in the way of treatment, he told me, other than behavior control with sedatives. He did give me the email of his fellow. A fellow is someone that further specializes after residency, such as a neurologist who wants to specialize in dementia care. When Michelle had been with my mom for nine months and the situation had become untenable, I wrote to him and asked if we could hospitalize her at UCLA until we found placement somewhere.

So, I took Michelle to the ER, where we waited five hours to get her admitted. Normally, the wait could be longer, but imagine a five-year-old with ADHD waiting five hours for anything! Watching my sister was like that. After a brief stint at UCLA, the skilled nursing facility (SNF) shuffle began! First, Michelle was placed somewhere in North Hollywood. The place was decent, but I foolishly thought I could get her placed closer to me on the West Side. I found a facility in Santa Monica, but that lasted only a week because they couldn't handle her. She constantly wandered in and out of rooms, picking up things that weren't hers. They sent her to Hollywood Presbyterian Hospital. I called every day, trying to get the provider to call me back. After several days, he finally did. He told me he had put Michelle on a medicine I knew had previously caused serious side effects for her. And he hadn't given her the medicine that was crucial for her sleep.

"If you had called me in the first place," I said, "this wouldn't have happened."

"I've been working as a psych NP (nurse practitioner) for many years," he snapped. "I know what I'm doing."

We continued to argue about her medications. He told me certain medications couldn't be mixed with others when absolutely, I knew they could. As a family physician and someone who had worked with PEH for sixteen years at that point, I was extremely comfortable treating psychiatric illnesses. In short, I knew my meds.

Michelle was placed again, but the new facility couldn't handle her, either. The cycle continued. In August of 2019, she became terribly ill with pneumonia. I thought she was going to die, but she recovered. The hospice nurse recommended we place her in rehabilitation because she had lost her ability to walk and feed herself.

Often, providers are more willing to recommend someone for rehab because Medicare pays $800 per day compared to custodial care, which is $200 a day. But when Michelle's ninety days of rehab were up, they said they'd move her to another SNF that would "better suit her needs."

A couple of weeks later, I received a message that Michelle would be picked up in forty-five minutes to be taken to the "Huntington Beach Health Care Facility." Later that night, the social worker from Huntington Beach Hospital left me a message asking more about Michelle's history. The admitting physician didn't call me. I called the social worker back. She had gone home, but I spoke with the charge nurse.

"Hi, my name is Susan Partovi. I am Michelle's sister and POA. Can you tell me why my sister was admitted, and what medications she's on?"

"I'm not allowed to give you any information over the phone."

"Why not? I'm her POA."

"We're a psychiatric floor. We don't acknowledge POA."

"But she's not a psychiatric patient," I said. "She has a medical disease."

"She was diagnosed with schizoaffective disorder and consented for treatment."

I shook my head. How can someone with a five-word vocabulary "consent" for her treatment? I'd heard about psychiatric medical personnel being unhelpful and even detrimental to patient care by obstructing family involvement. I asked to speak to the supervisor, who gave me the same robotic answers, all in the name of HIPAA (the Health Insurance Portability and Accountability Act of 1996).

These laws intended to protect sensitive patient health information from being disclosed without consent are often called upon for questionable reasons. Up to that point, I had never really read HIPAA laws, but I assumed they were different for psychiatric patients. Many friends and colleagues had reported horrible experiences with hospitals when their loved ones were hospitalized, with HIPAA being used as justification.

I asked the charge nurse to please have the attending physician call me so we could discuss Michelle's medications. That was a Thursday night. He never called me. On Monday, I called the social worker and spoke to her colleague, who was patient and compassionate to my circumstances. She said the attending physician, Dr. Johnson, was known to be very uncommunicative with family members. She said she'd make sure the nurse practitioner called me, and he did. We went over the medications, and he said he'd place Michelle back on the one she'd originally been taking.

My sister was at the hospital because the SNF hadn't been able to deal with her behavior. This is what we in the medical world call "a dump." Nursing homes can pick and choose the patients in their care. If a resident becomes a behavioral problem, instead of trying to address it, they can say "we can no longer meet her needs" and dump the patient into a hospital. Then, the hospital needs to find another SNF who will accept her.

The attending physician, Dr. Johnson, never called me. He ended up changing Michelle's medications again, without my consent or input. I read up on HIPAA on the Human Health Services website. Surprisingly, the laws were more generous and humane than I had imagined. Can medical personnel discuss medical information with family or friends if the patient is incapacitated? Yes, especially if it's in the best interest of the patient's care. Can medical personnel discuss information over the phone? Yes! Is there any difference with patients at a mental health facility? No, except for the sharing of psychotherapy notes.

It seemed to me there was much misinterpretation and misunderstanding of HIPAA laws. About a year and a half before, Michelle had suddenly become acutely altered and couldn't walk (eventually, we found out this was due to one of her medications causing severe sodium depletion, which can be deadly). The caretaker of her SNF had called 911, and Michelle was sent to Sherman Oaks Hospital. When I was alerted, I immediately called the ER, telling the nurse who answered I was Michelle's sister and POA.

He told me, "I cannot give any information over the phone. She's an adult and has rights."

"Actually, she isn't an adult," I answered. "She has a neurological disease that has rendered her like a five-year-old. And I am her POA."

He wouldn't budge. I called again and spoke to another nurse, who yelled at me. "I'm not going to risk my nursing license to go against HIPAA!"

Eventually, I spoke with the nursing director, who asked me to send a copy of the POA papers. She said she'd have the attending physician call me as soon as he or she could. The attending did call at midnight, apologizing for the inconvenience. I emailed her the POA papers and told her I wanted to make a formal complaint.

I had battled in the past with medical practitioners in the name of HIPAA. HIPPA, a federal law, and California's privacy laws say the exact same thing when it comes to incapacitated patients and/or psychiatric patients—except, the state laws dictate that ultimately, it's up to the decision of the medical staff! Many patients are being harmed by the inability of medical staff to read and correctly interpret these laws.

After my sister's most recent hospitalization, I researched suing Dr. Johnson and his hospital, but a colleague said it wouldn't go in my favor.

My sister, Michelle, was a caring high school teacher who related to her students and found fun ways to teach them French. She had an infectious giggle and loved to play the slot machines on her frequent trips to Las Vegas. In her early fifties, she started to exhibit abnormal behavior and show signs of dementia. Eventually, she was diagnosed with a deteriorating neurological disorder that affects behavior, memory, and speech. Michelle lived in Lancaster, about an hour-and-a-half drive from me and when her condition deteriorated and she lost her teaching job, suddenly, I had to take care of her from afar. Becoming someone's power of attorney and caregiver means taking care of a range of responsibilities. I had to advocate for her with medical professionals until we figured out what was going on with her. I hired a revolving cast of part-time caretakers—some great, some fraudulent and/or neglectful—and took care of her animals, her house, and her bills. For a while, I moved Michelle in with my mother, who already had twenty-four-hour caretakers because of inability to take care of herself due to Alzheimer's.

Taking care of both my sister and mother has been the most difficult and lonely experience of my life. In addition to handling the responsibilities of my own life, I dealt with doctors, psychiatrists, and a whole host of people in the financial realm—public aid, banking, etc.—but ultimately, the decisions about how best to care for them rested solely on my shoulders. My father had been gone for years, and my half-brother had died in 2018 of a sudden heart attack.

Michelle died in April, 2022, of pneumonia. It was her third bout with pneumonia, and I instructed the nursing home to give her palliative care. My thinking was to let her be at peace. I visited her the day before she passed. She had her hands folded over her chest. She opened her eyes for a few seconds, took a sip of juice, and closed her eyes again. She was, indeed, very much at peace. She had been in six different nursing homes, but in the last place for two years. Overall, it had been a nightmare and a near-constant strain. Being someone's caretaker comes with a rotating range of emotions, from guilt, to sadness, to a feeling of being overwhelmed, to hopelessness and back to guilt again.

So, umpteen years after I met Antonio and his brother, and years after taking over my sister Michelle's care, I have decided that, no, Antonio wasn't neglected. His brother was doing the best he could with what he knew—and perhaps, with what he had. Maybe in some ways, he was Antonio's hero. Not everyone who can't take care of themselves has a brother like Antonio. With more assistance and intervention, Antonio's brother could have provided a higher level of care. Taking care of another person—managing their physical and mental needs, and assuming control of their practical affairs—is a stressful and overwhelming task. And some people don't have anyone to step up for them. As a society, we should think about those who don't have a brother, sister, or loved one bringing them to the doctor or looking after them when they need it most. They usually end up on the streets or in jail. This would certainly have been the case with my sister if I had not stepped in. This is part of the reason why I see everyone with special needs, everyone living in the streets without care, as family. I see it as my duty, as our duty, to care for those who cannot care for themselves. Not everyone agrees with this sentiment, but I know our society would thrive on these ideals. When we see others as "we" and not "them," we thrive. Or maybe that's just the renegade in me.

5

NEC FASC

Leonard walked into the clinic in Skid Row. "Hey Doc," he said breathlessly. "I'm glad you're here."

He looked horrible. Leonard was a big, buff man—"prison-buff" we'd call it. His muscles had muscles.

I started working at the Needle Exchange at Homeless Health Care Los Angeles (HHCLA) in 2004—sometimes four days a week, sometimes once or twice a week, depending on my other clinic responsibilities. After my residency and six years on faculty at Harbor-UCLA, I became disillusioned by the politics of academia and treated patients full-time at the Venice Family Clinic. But soon, I discovered I couldn't handle full-time patient care. It was too stressful, seeing patients all day, every day! It felt like being on a never-ending conveyor belt. I transitioned to part-time and looked for other opportunities. While teaching at UCLA's medical school, I was introduced to HHCLA by a colleague. At the time, she was the medical director, and she needed a doctor to treat wounds at the Needle Exchange. I thought it would be a great experience, add to my routine patient care, and further my goals to work with the impoverished and people experiencing homelessness.

At the Needle Exchange, I mostly treated injection drug users with abscesses and wounds, but I also considered the clinic to be a safety net facility, where I tried to connect patients with appropriate resources. Because access to health care was extremely limited before expanded Medicaid, I tried to patchwork each patient's chronic conditions until I could get them into one of the overcrowded free clinics in the area. The neglect of chronic conditions is the main reason PEH have a life expectancy of forty-seven years.

Injection drug users were (and still are) treated very poorly in ERs and hospitals. Often, they're judged for their drug use and looked down upon when seeking help for chronic, often severe wound infections from using needles. Patients like Leonard felt this disdain down to their core and were desperate for help. When HHCLA started offering medical services downtown, I was the doctor to care for them. Leonard was a heroin user and a regular.

At the Needle Exchange, the clinic was a small room inside our storefront facility. Prior to Obamacare, we had to keep supplies of medications for our patients—most of whom didn't have any sort of medical insurance. Sometimes, when I didn't see Leonard for a while, I'd wonder, *Is he in jail? Did he get clean? Is he dead?* Those were the usual options for our missing regulars.

When Leonard came in, he was wearing a hospital band on his right wrist; beads of sweat had formed on his forehead. I noticed immediately that his right arm was bright red, twice the size of his other arm. It sprouted from his tank top like an infected tree trunk.

"What's going on, Leonard?" I asked, trying to sound calm when I was really going into "something's-fucking-wrong-here" mode. In these situations, I may appear calm, but my brain goes into full gear, running through potential causes, diagnoses, and remedies.

He looked at me with brown eyes full of fear. "I was at county for twenty-four hours. I couldn't wait anymore. I'm real bad, Doc. I knew you'd know what to do."

Fuck. I only swear when it absolutely fits the occasion, and the appearance of Leonard's arm was definitely curse-worthy. By "county," he meant the Los Angeles County USC hospital. The county hospitals were always overtaxed with uninsured patients. Back then, people could wait for days to receive care in the ER. I stuck a thermometer in his mouth and took his heart rate, which was rocketing to 140. His temperature was 102. I helped him take off his tank top.

Fuck. His huge, fire-red, tautly swollen arm fanned flames of redness onto his chest. This was necrotizing fasciitis. We call it "Nec Fasc," a rare, flesh-eating bacteria that can develop from skin breach caused by injection use. And it's usually deadly, within hours. I had to think fast.

I should call 911. But if I do, they'll take him back to county where he might be placed back into the never-ending line of people waiting to be seen. He'll die for sure.

I decided to give him four Bactrim, an oral antibiotic, and two shots of ceftriaxone, another antibiotic. That's all I had available at the clinic. While he rested, I called Harbor-UCLA's ER. It was a county hospital, too, but I had connections. I still knew everyone from when I'd been an attending physician there and moonlighting in the ER, treating the less urgent patients.

As I gave Leonard the second shot of ceftriaxone, someone answered the phone. I heard the usual clamor of the emergency room in the background. "Yes, hello, this is Dr. Partovi. Who's the attending on duty right now?"

The nurse put me on hold and in a couple of minutes, Dr. Gauche picked up. *Thank God*. Dr. Marianne Gauche was an attending physician at Harbor's ER when I was a resident and later, an attending myself in the family medicine department. She was smart, down-to-earth, and truly caring. A good doctor! I knew she'd understand my need to be a renegade in this case.

"Marianne, it's Susan Partovi. I'm at the Needle Exchange, and I have a guy in his forties with Nec Fasc. He came here after waiting twenty-four hours at Big County (our name for the LAC/USC hospital). If I call 911, they'll take him back. He's alert, but his temperature is 102 and pulse is 140. Blood pressure is okay. I'm going to drive him to Harbor. Oh, and Marianne, he's dope sick."

When someone who uses opiates takes a break, even a short one, they develop withdrawal symptoms such as abdominal pain, vomiting, diarrhea, severe pain, and anxiety. This is "dope sick"—basically, the worst flu you can imagine. In fact, most chronic opiate users continue using to avoid dealing with these withdrawal symptoms. Most of the time, when someone is hospitalized for these severe symptoms and not given adequate opiates to alleviate and treat their pain, they'll leave the hospital. I'd had patients die because the doctors wouldn't treat their dope sickness, causing them to leave "against medical advice." It was important that Leonard didn't leave because, if he did, he would die.

She paused for a moment. "I'll be waiting in triage with morphine ready."

Yes!

I patted Leonard on the leg. "Let's go for a ride."

"Really?" Gingerly, he scooted off the bed.

"Yes, really."

Minutes later, we were in my 2000 Toyota 4Runner and whizzing down the freeway. Every now and then, I looked over at Leonard's massively swollen arm and swore I could feel the heat it was giving off.

He sat with his hands resting in his lap, unfazed by the turn of events. "Nice car, Doc."

"Thanks." I shot down the 110 and turned off Carson Avenue, parking in the "Emergency Patients Only" spot. I grabbed my badge from the glove compartment.

The security guard's eyebrows rose as we approached the automatic door. I flashed my identification and said, "He's with me." Inside, we went straight to triage, weaving through the people standing around, the cots in the hallway, and doctors and nurses buzzing about. Marianne saw us and came around the nurses' station desk pushing a wheelchair. She took Leonard back, and I could finally take a deep breath.

Now that's the way it's done! Marianne and I were on the same page. Had it been any other attending, it may not have been so easy. She trusted my assessment and I trusted she would take care of my patient "in the back." That night, he had surgery, and he spent three months in the hospital receiving multiple skin grafts. Then, he was transferred to the county rehabilitation hospital, Rancho Los Amigos, for six months.

Before expanded Medicaid, most people qualifying for the federal poverty level did not receive Medicaid. The criteria stated that you had to have certain diseases such as breast cancer, cervical cancer, or kidney failure needing dialysis, or patients needed to meet the federal poverty level and have children under the age of eighteen. Then, the children and parents would be covered—if they were legally documented or citizens. This left out a lot of folks. Thus, community clinics had to bear the brunt of providing care and most of these were nonprofits relying on contributions. It could take anywhere from nine to eighteen months to get an appointment with a specialist at a county facility. Often, we would send people to the ER so that they could receive care sooner. This, of course, meant that the ERs were full of people who couldn't afford primary or specialty care. The ensuing backup could result in patients waiting for days.

Los Angeles County has many outpatient and county clinics, and four county hospitals. Decades ago, the county developed a safety net care system, intended for people who don't have medical insurance. It's free care, but the wait times for appointments and treatment can be staggering. After expanded Medicaid, mostly the undocumented comprise the "safety net" population. With the reduction of numbers, the wait for both primary care and specialty clinics has shortened. Some counties don't have a safety net system at all. For example, there are no county hospitals in Orange County or San Diego County. Heck, there are no public medical facilities in all of Nevada! I am so thankful for expanded Medicaid and affordable coverage for many Americans— well, in most states. It continues to shock me that people are often forced to choose between their livelihood and their health. And to think, some people want to revoke the advances made by Obamacare to provide healthcare for our most needy, with no alternate plan.

When I finally saw Leonard again at the Needle Exchange, he had lost probably sixty pounds. Most of the muscle from his upper arm and chest had been removed, and he couldn't move that arm much due to the taught scar tissue. And yet, he was smiling.

"What's up Leonard?" I asked, my smile matching his.

With a lollipop in his mouth, he smiled even wider. "Just came by to thank you for saving my life, Doc!"

I looked into his eyes, still brown but bright and clear now. "Any time, Leonard. Any time."

Leonard did return to the streets and started using heroin again. I remember seeing him and thinking again about how skinny he had become. Eventually, he was incarcerated, and he used that time to get clean and stay clean. I last saw him in 2015, and he was housed and still free from drugs.

In 2006, I became the medical director for HHCLA. I run the urgent care clinic and am known as the queen of abscess care. We handle a lot of wounds and abscesses—a result of injection drug use— but we also address acute care issues such as mental illness, vaccinations, and detox treatment with Suboxone. Because I had treated Leonard for minor issues in the past but never judged him for his drug use, he knew he could trust me with a life and death illness. Most people would not have done what I did for Leonard. I tell this story not to boast about how badass I am, because sometimes, my renegade attempts fail. But when life and death or severe suffering is involved, I'm going to do whatever it takes to take care of my family. Leonard is family. Treating patients like Leonard can often start with something simple that has the potential to develop into something severe—or as it did in his case—deadly.

6

TRAGICARE

FIRST PATIENT OF THE DAY: WOKE UP WITH DECREASED hearing in one ear. Because she's a musician, she was extremely concerned. Her ears looked normal. Referral to ENT (the ear/nose/throat doctor), this week.

Next patient: Worsening back pain radiating down the leg. She'd had an injury the year before and had been dealing with on and off pain. The neurological exam was normal—thus, not an emergency. Pain medications prescribed, MRI ordered for next week, and follow-up with an orthopedic surgeon and a spine specialist to boot. Most likely, she had a slipped disc, but I wanted to find out the severity and whether the specialist would recommend any procedures.

Another patient: Blood present in his ear and because he'd had perforated ear drums in the past, he wanted to make sure he didn't have another one. Nope, the ear drum was intact. Small laceration in the canal and advise to call his ENT for evaluation.

Ahhhhh, the feeling of working with insured patients! I was moonlighting at a private practice's urgent care, and the clients all had great coverage. Need a study? No problem. A specialist? How does next week sound? There's nothing like being able to provide the medical care a patient needs! But that's not how it is for the uninsured.

Before ObamaCare, treating the uninsured at my community clinic, Saban in Hollywood, was a completely different story. One patient I saw had anemia. His chart showed three positive stool cards (a screening for colon cancer), eighteen months prior.

"Have you had a colonoscopy yet?" I asked. The chart also showed he had lost fifteen pounds in the last six months.

He hadn't. I noted that he'd been *referred* for the colonoscopy, also eighteen months ago. When I asked the referral coordinator for the status, she said "still pending." Because I had worked at one of the county hospitals, I knew some tricks to get patients seen. I called the back line for the Endoscopy Suite and asked to speak with one of the fellows. I told him the story.

"Send him to the emergency room," he recommended.

"But he's stable. He just needs an urgent colonoscopy."

"No such thing," he replied. But he took the patient's name and number and said he'd try to get him in within a month.

Another patient I saw had torn her biceps tendon over a year before. "I'm still waiting to see orthopedics," she told me. I checked the status: "still pending." I examined her biceps muscle, now beginning to atrophy. If I had seen her initially, I would have sent her to the county emergency room, knowing that it takes over a year to get an orthopedics appointment at county.

When I send patients to the emergency room, I tell them, "You'll wait twenty-four to thirty-six hours to been seen, but if it's serious enough, you'll see an orthopedist in the ER. At the very least, the ER will refer you to their orthopedics clinic within a few weeks."

Perhaps you are starting to see why the ERs were so crowded before Obamacare. Orthopedics was a special case because there wasn't one Orthopedic Surgeon who would take MediCal. So even when a patient had MediCal, all orthopedic problems went through the county.

I saw a man in his forties who had what seemed like an enlarged lymph node on one side. It was grape-sized and had been there for about two years. He was not a smoker or drinker (both increase the risk for head and neck cancer), so I ordered a tuberculosis test and referred him to an ENT, knowing it would be a six-month wait. He came back in one month—TB test negative, but by then, the mass was the size of a golf ball and had grown rock hard. So, I gave him the speech. "I'm going to send you to the ER, because you can't wait any longer for a biopsy and they are the only ones who can get you into an ENT within a week. You could wait over twenty-four hours, so bring a coat, food, a book and just be patient."

I saw a thirty-something-year-old man who'd had an inguinal hernia (a weakening of the muscles resulting in a bulge, in the groin area) for a couple of years. He wanted surgery. But it wasn't an emergency. "I'll refer you," I said, "but it'll take six to nine months to get an appointment. Then it will take a year, or two, before you get the actual surgery."

I can't imagine having to wait so long for health care. Some people will say, "If we have Universal Health Care, this is what it will be like. It will be like the county but for everyone." But that's not correct. The county wasn't providing universal health care. It provided *Safety Net* care—enormous difference! Safety net care tries to pick up the slack to provide healthcare to patients who otherwise couldn't get anything but truly emergent care. And even emergent care wasn't always available for the uninsured. In the 1980s, a group of young doctors in training noticed that when patients were transferred from private hospitals to public hospitals for emergent conditions, they would arrive dead. So EMTALA (Emergency Medical Treatment & Labor Act) makes it mandatory for every emergency room in the U.S. to attend to every patient that crosses its threshold irrespective of ability to pay and to provide emergent and hospital care if needed.

Let me give you an example of Universal Health Care provided by California: prenatal and maternity Care. Before the 1990s, if a pregnant woman didn't have medical insurance, she was required to deliver at county hospitals. I started my training at a county hospital in the mid-90s and remember hearing stories about how it used to be—deliveries in hallways because of overcrowding, NICUs (Neonatal Intensive Care Unit) packed with premature and sick infants because there was no prenatal care. And then California decided this type of care was intolerable. In our state, all pregnant women without insurance were given MediCal and low and behold, the county delivery rooms became relatively quiet. The NICUs emptied. Women received prenatal care and could deliver at UCLA, Cedars-Sinai, or any hospital they chose. Obstetrical and infant mortality plummeted. The hospitals were happy because they were getting paid, and there were no longer waiting lists for prenatal care or overcrowded delivery rooms. You see, there were plenty of providers and hospitals available to take care of these patients.

It's still a waiting game for the uninsured in this county, but the odds have improved.

* * *

The resident at Saban Community Clinic presented a woman's case. "I've got a fifty-one-year-old woman with diabetes, hypertension, and hyperlipidemia (high cholesterol), complaining of chest pain for the past couple of months. The pain is on her right side and radiates down the arm. The pain isn't related to activity, and when she gets it, she also experiences nausea and vomiting."

When a patient presents with chest pain, there are two things that help us decide whether to pursue a workup for angina (chest pain caused by the lack of oxygen to the heart muscle, usually caused by blockage of the arteries that bring oxygenated blood to the heart muscle). First, we learn about the chest pain itself—what we call "the story." In the case of angina, chest pain or pressure in the mid-chest or left side occurs with activity or stress—anything that increases the heart rate. This pain can last several minutes (five to twenty, typically), radiates down the left arm, and is relieved with rest. The typical concomitant symptoms are shortness of breath, nausea and/or vomiting, sweating, and a feeling of "doom."

Second, we look at one's risk factors for heart disease. These factors are a known history of a previous heart attack, diabetes, a family history of a first-degree relative who suffered a heart attack at an early age (less than sixty), hypertension, and hyperlipidemia. If the patient has significant risk factors or "the story" is typical for angina, we pursue the workup for angina.

This patient was a fifty-one-year-old woman with pain on the right side unassociated with activity. However, she had many risk factors, so a workup for angina was justified. We ordered an EKG (electrocardiogram) to check whether she'd had a heart attack and found no evidence. But when we compared it to an old EKG, there were some significant changes that could be consistent with injury.

I called our referral coordinator, "What's quicker, a stress echocardiogram or a nuclear medicine scan?" Both show whether activity causes decreased oxygen to the heart or increased heart rate—thus indicating a blockage in a cardiac artery.

"Both are the same," she said. "Nine to twelve months."

You see, this patient had come to a community clinic in Los Angeles. Normally, a doctor's decisions would relate only to what is the best approach, medically, for the patient. But we have a host of other concerns. This patient was uninsured. We had sent all our cardiac testing to one of LA's county hospitals, the only place they could go for specialty care. And of course, they were usually in for a long wait.

"We have another source that allows one treadmill test per month," the coordinator added, "but only Dr. Smith can approve it."

I looked at her, wondering how we would determine whether this patient deserved the treadmill test more than any other patient from our four medical sites.

She nodded. "All right, I'll give you the referral. We have one open for September."

"I'll take it!"

Still, it was several weeks away. We added medication to lower the patient's heart rate and open the vessels. We'd treat her as if she had angina, hoping she wouldn't have a heart attack before the test.

Later the same day, another patient with hypertension and a family history of a heart attack came in. This woman was fifty-two, and her mother had died at fifty-one of a heart attack! The patient had been experiencing chest pain in her mid-chest after fifteen minutes of walking, which was relieved with rest. Her "story" lined up with angina, all the risk factors were there. But she also had no insurance.

I had already used my one ticket for a special treadmill test. This patient's EKG looked okay (no previous heart attack, injury, or arrythmias), so I put in a referral for a stress echocardiogram, knowing it would take nine to twelve months. I wrote prescriptions for the same medications as the previous patient, adding baby aspirin and nitroglycerin for use when rest didn't relieve her chest pain. None of these would, however, prevent death from a heart attack. Before she left, we gave her a list of precautions about when she should go to the emergency room.

The same day, I saw a third patient with chest pains. This one was a fifty-one-year-old, uninsured man with hypertension. For the past couple of months, he had experienced pain with walking, relieved with rest! Really?! His EKG looked okay, so we started the same medications and filled out the form for a study (to check for arterial blockages) that may happen sometime next year. We gave him the same ER precautions.

In 2012, before expanded Medicaid, the number of uninsured in the United States was up to fifty-two million individuals! Twenty-two thousand people died every year because they were uninsured. British Medical Journal (BMJ) cited in 2008 that twenty-six thousand Americans died each year due to lack of health insurance. I just gave you three examples of patients who could have died due to being uninsured. Heart disease is the number one cause of death in the United States. In 2018, the American Heart Association stated that 7.3 million Americans with cardiovascular disease were uninsured and far less likely to receive timely, appropriate, and adequate medical care. This, of course, leads to worse outcomes, including an increased mortality rate. People who are underinsured have the same problems. And studies have shown that individuals without health insurance, especially those with heart disease, stroke, high blood pressure or diabetes, experience a dramatic improvement in health when they become eligible for Medicare coverage at age sixty-five.

What will it take to show those against health care for all that everyone in the U.S. needs quality and timely health care to decrease mortality and improve quality of life? Maybe those who want to cut access to health care don't care about poor people. Possibly, they're concerned about the fiscal impact. On the economic side, it's more cost efficient to provide health care for all. Studies show that the uninsured use the emergency room more frequently for non-emergent care, causing hospitals to go into debt or worse, close altogether. Furthermore, the uninsured take longer to seek emergent care, thus presenting to the hospital in worse conditions and requiring longer hospital stays. This strains the safety net even more. In my eyes, it's a moral injustice that some individuals must risk their health by avoiding primary care and delaying emergent care—but at least we can all agree that providing access to quality and timely care saves communities money. If I can't convince people to care about poor people, I can at least make an economic case.

7

ELBOW FRACTURE; BIG DUDE

I SAW A HOMELESS PATIENT AT THE NEEDLE EXCHANGE. HE was a small, Latino guy, in his fifties but looked older.

My assistant handed me the chart. "His arm was run over by an SUV," she said.

"What?!" Sure enough, his entire right arm was bruised and deformed. It was obvious that his distal humerus, the elbow, was fractured.

"How did this happen?" I asked.

He looked up at me with matter-of-fact brown eyes. "Well, I was sleeping in my sleeping bag in the alley—"

Before he could finish his sentence, the picture came to my mind. *Oh my God! His arm didn't get run over by an SUV. HE was run over by an SUV while sleeping in the alley!*

I watched his face. "Did the driver stop?"

Cradling his injured arm with the other one, he shrugged. "No."

* * *

That same day, I saw this big dude. He had a spike piercing his bottom lip. He was at the clinic for an abscess on his arm. He showed me the bag full of medicine he took for seizures, hypertension, and mental health problems.

"Where did you get these medications?" I asked.

"Jail."

"When did you get out?"

"Three weeks ago."

"How long were you in?"

"Three years."

"You were clean for three years?"

"Yeah."

"What got you using again?"

"Coming back to this hellhole."

He meant Skid Row. If you are homeless when released from jail, they give you two hundred dollars, your belongings, and one month's supply of medications. Then you're released to the streets.

"Any family?" I asked.

"Nope."

I referred him to the L.A. Christian Health Center in the hopes he'd follow up on his high blood pressure and seizure disorder, and to Downtown Mental Health for his psychiatric condition.

I doubted he would go. He had other, basic priorities to deal with every day. In jail, at least he had a place to sleep, eat, shower, and get his medications.

I wondered which was worse—jail or the streets?

8

FREE WILL

THE PHONE RANG AT 3 A.M.

"Dr. Partovi," a woman's voice said, "I'm calling to let you know that William expired this morning."

It was late 2006, and I had met William six months earlier while working at the Venice Family Clinic. I remembered his loud, childlike voice. "No, no! I'm not going back to the hospital!"

He'd just been released from the hospital for congestive heart failure, and I had told him I wanted to refer him to a cardiologist.

Originally from Canada, William had moved to Los Angeles to get a master's degree in education. He lived by himself in an apartment in Brentwood. His sister lived in Canada, and he had a niece in New Jersey. He owned several boats in Marina del Rey, renting them out for income. He was sixty-one and three years before, he had suffered a heart attack and stroke. He dressed casually, in T-shirts and pants that were a little too big.

When I talked with him that first time, it was obvious he could no longer care for himself. He sounded like a stubborn, whining toddler. Although he could answer most questions, his judgment was extremely limited. And if he couldn't answer a question, he'd say, "My memory's not good." I wondered about his mental state.

The woman friend who'd brought him assured me that she would take care of him. I didn't know the nature of their relationship and didn't ask.

When I was growing up, there were many rules in my house, and most of them didn't make any sense to me. "You don't wear shorts on the bus," "You don't 'date' anyone except your dad or grandpa," "No junk food allowed in the house," "Kids can't use a camera," "Take a shower once a week," "Bedtime is eight o'clock!" I hated rules and couldn't wait until I was an adult so I could do whatever I wanted. If you had asked me about free will when I was a child, it would have had something to do with wearing what I wanted, going where I wanted whenever I wanted, and using my own judgment to make decisions. This is the whole idea of adulthood, being in charge! But what if someone's judgment becomes impaired? Do we still grant them the privilege of free will?

I saw William in my continuity clinic, which provides continuous care for chronic conditions; he came every two weeks or so. As time went on, the woman stopped coming, and another friend, Mike, would accompany him. Mike organized medications in a pillbox for William, made sure he had food in the refrigerator, and helped him pay his bills.

I prescribed William low doses of a sedative in addition to his cardiac medications, to help with his agitation. During one of his appointments, I asked a volunteer psychiatrist at the clinic to chat with him for a while. When the doctor sat down, he asked where she was from.

"Israel," she told him.

His eyes lit up. "Oh, Israel. I've been there before. I used to work in Europe and would visit. I loved it there."

For the first time, he spoke in a deep, confident, masculine voice as he reminisced about the past. I had never seen this lucid side of him, this glimpse into his former self. Though he and the psychiatrist bonded, he never followed up with her office at the county mental health clinic, despite numerous attempts by both of us to get him there.

She diagnosed him with dementia, a result of his previous stroke.

When my own mother began to decline due to Alzheimer's, I had to step in, against her free will, and hire around-the-clock caretakers for her. They reminded her to shower, gave her medications, took her to buy groceries, and prepared and served meals. At first, she protested their involvement, but they were patient, working with her gently and with respect. I took over her finances, only to find a complete disaster. She hadn't paid her property taxes in five years; in fact, had I not stepped in when I did, she would have lost her home.

For a few months, William remained relatively healthy. During one of his regular appointments, Mike confessed that he had only met William recently when he bought one of his boats. He had been trying to help but couldn't continue being so involved and bringing him to the clinic.

I told him I understood.

After that, William still showed up for periodic appointments, but his health began to deteriorate. He began to look unkempt and wore dirty clothes that seemed to get looser and looser. He once admitted to me, "I can't take care of myself. They turned off my gas and electricity. I can ask Mike to be my conservator." This was in 2006. I didn't know then what it took to conserve someone. In 2009, I had to investigate conservatorship to take over caring for my mom.

I called Adult Protective Services to see if they could help, but he wouldn't let them in when they came knocking on his door. They're not allowed to force themselves into someone's home. When I called them to follow up, they said, "He's got a personality problem. We can't help him." He missed a clinic visit, and I called to see what had happened. He had driven himself to the emergency room because of abdominal pain. Most likely, it was angina, related to his uncontrolled heart failure. While he was there, I spoke to the hospitalist who was taking care of him and asked for a psychiatric consultation. If William were deemed incapable of making his own decisions, he could be placed in a long-term facility.

After the consultation, I spoke with the psychiatrist. He claimed William knew his name and where he lived, and that he was very insistent about *not* being placed in a long-term facility. According to this doctor's assessment, William was "fully competent."

"But he can't take care of himself," I replied. "He doesn't have food, he can't pay his bills, he won't take his medications!"

"It's his free will to not take his medications," the psychiatrist said.

Mike picked William up from the hospital and took him home. A "sitter" from the hospital (someone assigned to sit with agitated or upset patients and assist them) took pity on William and decided to become his home health caretaker. She told me that his apartment was unlivable and filthy. She cleaned it, washed his clothes, and stocked the fridge.

The next day, she called me in a panic. "Dr. Partovi, he won't take his medications. Sometimes, he'll take the car without telling me. I thought I took his keys away, but he had another set."

She called again to say that William had become verbally abusive, which she didn't deserve after everything she'd done for him. She had lasted only three days.

I never did like my own mother much. I remember wanting to sleep with my parents when I was six years old. She insisted that children didn't belong in a couple's bed, but my father told her to let me in. The next day, she said "That's the last time I do that! You tossed and turned and kicked me all night long." I still sleep like that, I think. When I was growing up, I often felt like I was the parent—wiser, stronger, more "normal" than my mom. The child in me would say the woman who bore me didn't deserve to take up the space on this page. The adult me recognizes that she was a shitty mother, but she'd had a shitty life and did her best. She didn't share much of her life willingly, but as I grew older, the parts I was able to learn shed light on how she became the way she was.

Mike was still trying to help William. A few days after my conversation with the sitter from the hospital, he called to tell me that when he'd gone to William's apartment, he found him lying naked on the couch. William had said he couldn't find anything to wear.

I decided I would hospitalize him at the county hospital, where I had staff privileges. Once he was there, I'd try to get another psychiatric consultation. Mike agreed to take him, but William refused to go.

In the weeks following, his health deteriorated more, because he wouldn't take his medications. But he'd still show up for his appointments, which were now weekly. He couldn't tell me why he wouldn't take his medicine, but he'd say, "I promise, I'm going to do better." Like a three-year old promising not to hit his sister.

One day, I received a call from his landlord. "William looks very sick," he said, "but he won't go to the hospital."

When I called, William was breathless on the phone.

"What's going on?" I asked.

"Nothing. Everything—is—fine." He took a breath between each word.

"Your landlord is worried about you. He says you're sick."

He coughed and wheezed. "I just have a cold."

"It sounds like you're having difficulty breathing," I said. "Just go to the hospi—"

Before I finished, he hung up on me.

I called the Psychiatric Emergency Response Team (aka the PET team), who claimed they couldn't force themselves into someone's home without consent. I knew William wouldn't let them in. They recommended I ask the police to do a courtesy check-in. But they, too, said they weren't allowed to force entry.

Over the months I saw him at the clinic, William had gained over fifty pounds in fluid. He was bloated and short of breath. Again and again, I begged him to go to the hospital, but he vehemently refused each time.

"Do you want to die?" I'd ask, exasperated.

"No, no, I don't want to die," he'd tell me. No matter how often I explained, he couldn't understand that not taking his medications was slowly killing him.

The Monday after he hung up on me, he came to the clinic complaining of chest pain. I wasn't there, but another attending physician evaluated him and called the paramedics. When they came, he refused to go to the hospital.

Once again, the paramedics proclaimed him competent, saying they couldn't take him if he refused. The attending called the PET Team, who thought his condition was medical and not psychiatric. They showed up eventually, but William had already left the clinic.

He returned that night to see me during my evening shift. I decided to forgo the dramatics of the PET team, and I called yet another new roommate, John, to take William to the hospital. John picked him up but called the next day to say that William had refused to go to the hospital again.

A few days later, John called again, this time in a panic. "Dr. Partovi, William looks horrible. He can't get off the couch and he's hallucinating. He's barely breathing!"

"Call 911!" I said.

I could hear hesitancy in his silence. "I know you don't want to betray him," I said, "but he's going to die on that couch if you don't."

He said he would call.

I called the ER once William arrived. While I was talking to the physician on duty, I could hear his loud, boyish cries, "No, no, no!"

"We'll get him tuned up," the ER physician assured me. "By the way, what's his code status?"

I was stunned. I had never discussed code status or advanced directives with William. Code status refers to what emergent services a person wishes to receive if their heart or breathing stops. Do we resuscitate, or not? So, when "Code Blue" is called, the clinicians know how to respond. Full code is when the team responds to fully resuscitate the patient with CPR, intubation, cardioversion, and medications. Or a patient can be classified as "DNR" (do not resuscitate). I regularly instruct medical students about advanced directive, and yet, it had never entered my mind, despite all the times I had told William he would die if he didn't take his medication.

"Full code," I responded.

I walked slowly to my car, contemplating the thought of William dying. I shook it off and went home. I wasn't sure what else I could have done. Later that night, I got the call—the dreaded, 3 a.m. call.

Beginning in 1967 when state laws were adopted to protect the right to refuse psychiatric treatment, and during the deinstitutionalization of psychiatric patients that escalated throughout the twentieth century and into this one, it has become increasingly difficult to involuntarily hospitalize the mentally ill or mentally impaired. The police, paramedics and physicians all know the basic criterion: "If the patient is at risk of harming him/herself or others," they can be involuntarily hospitalized.

But what is harm? Wasn't William harming himself by refusing medical care under the guise of "free will?" Now in retrospect, William's behavior wasn't due to mental illness, but to dementia. Dementia is a brain disease, like mental illness, but comes on later in life and also causes one to lose the ability to make rational decisions such as caring for one's bills or health. However, when there isn't a family member advocating for the patient, providers will often confound dementia and mental illness and erroneously fall back on state laws of civil rights and free will as defined in each state's code for a "mental disorder." If an inability to care for oneself is proven to have a medical cause, it is often easier to navigate as a caretaker. However, paramedics, law enforcement and even doctors frequently don't know the differences between diagnoses and the laws around forced treatment. In fact, I hadn't realized that his cognitive decline was due to dementia until my psychiatrist friend made the diagnosis.

Around this same time, I'd see a man in Santa Monica every day, all day, sitting on the same stoop. He had matted hair down to his hips, long nails, and a honeydew-melon-sized hernia easily visible under his filthy clothes. He was homeless, quite harmless, and very sweet, but he refused anything from outreach workers. Food, water, hygiene kits, socks—all rebuffed. Sometimes, he would accept cigarettes or coffee. Wasn't he harming himself? Wasn't it harmful to live on the streets unbathed, without medical attention for a chronic condition?

When I started taking care of my mother and her affairs, I realized that she bought into every scam that came her way. "Pay twenty dollars to get your prize money of three million!" She spent money on things she saw on television; she had three contraptions guaranteed to give her a "six pack" abdomen. She had creams, weight loss gimmicks, and other exercise equipment she never used. In those first years, we were still able to go out to dinner every couple of weeks, see movies, go shopping. But taking care of her was a full-time preoccupation, and her condition and needs were always changing. If she hadn't had children or someone else to help, she could have become homeless and wouldn't have survived long. My mother and I had a complicated relationship, and becoming her caregiver had its challenging moments. I tried to respect her pride, but when it came to her physical well-being, free will went out the window. Because no matter what, she was my mother. Despite unresolved issues or tense exchanges, I had no choice but to step in and exert my will over hers. I had to decide what was best for her because over time, she lost the ability to make rational decisions for herself.

As it stands, the law allows people the free will to refuse treatment unless certain legal criteria are met or a judge decides that forced treatment is necessary. As someone on the front lines of treating the mentally ill, I would like to see the law take better care of people like William and the man with the hernia. Perhaps the issue confronting us is not about free will at all. It could reflect our own disinclination as citizens and taxpayers to fund more treatment facilities, counselors, and hospitals for the mentally ill. "Free will" is cited as an excuse for insufficient care and resources for the mentally ill. Holding too strongly to the sanctity of free will is harming our mentally ill and deafening us to this reality. If society could envision every individual as a potential mother, father, brother, sister, cousin, aunt, grandparent, etc., then we could see our way to making sure everyone is well cared for, like my mom was.

9

FREE WILL, PART 2

"DID YOU BRING THE STAPLE REMOVER?" SUSIE, AN OUTREACH worker for the Ocean Park Community Center (OPCC, now "The People Concern") in Santa Monica, waited for my answer. She wore jeans and a sweatshirt, no makeup, and her shoulder-length hair in a neat ponytail. She was a go-getter. She knew her beat and how to incentivize her clients!

I was the street medicine doc for the Venice Family Clinic (VFC). In 2007, we had started pairing up with OPCC to address the medical concerns of those living on the streets, hoping to woo them into utilizing our services. From the first day I started this type of work, I began to realize how many PEH were severely mentally ill—to the point where they couldn't truly take care of themselves.

"Staple remover," I repeated hesitantly. "Yeah. Who's it for?"

"Bobby," she said. "He was mugged a couple of weeks ago. Hit over the head with a brick. We finally talked him into going to the emergency room. They put forty staples in his head!"

"Did they hospitalize him?"

"He refused."

Bobby was a homeless man whose regular spot was a stoop outside a convenience store two miles from the VFC. His dreadlocks, caked with a black substance, hung down to his knees. Was it grease, oil, dirt? It was hard to tell. He never bathed, and his fingernails were several inches long. He had lost one eye somehow, and a honeydew-melon-sized hernia clearly bulged underneath his filthy pants.

Along with an intern, I went to locate Bobby in the hopes of taking out his staples. We found him at his usual spot on the stoop. He looked up at us with his one good eye and slowly stood up. I decided his hernia was actually watermelon sized. "How's your head, Bobby?" I asked.

"It's okay," he responded, almost singing, giving every syllable the same length of note.

"How about I take your staples out?"

"It's okay, I'm okay."

I was determined. "The staples need to come out, Bobby."

"Staples? I was only in the hallway of the hospital for a few minutes." He shook his head, and his dreads swayed. "They didn't do anything to me. I'm okay," he sang again.

I stood my ground.

He looked up at me, and his face changed. "I guess you can do it if you want to."

I raised my eyebrows at the young, wide-eyed intern. I felt like I'd been given the keys to the city! Immediately, I took the prized tool—the staple remover—from my backpack of medical supplies and leaned over to begin. After removing each one as gently as possible, I'd ask Bobby if he was okay.

"I'm okay, ow! It's okay." He resumed his chant while rocking back and forth, which made my job slightly more difficult.

The locals all knew Bobby. As we took out his staples, people would walk by and comment. "Thank goodness, he's finally getting those out!" or "Lookin' good, Bobby!" A man in a wheelchair rolled up. "Bless you!" he said.

I had spoken to others about Bobby. Chief Davis of the Santa Monica Fire Department said his entire department had known him for years. Everyone described him as a gentle, shy man. They had tried to give Bobby all sorts of things, especially around Christmas time, but he would only take coffee or cigarettes.

Susie also knew him well. She said that Bobby usually wanted to be left alone and rarely accepted handouts. Most likely, he was schizophrenic, as those afflicted often prefer to be solitary. His brother, who lived in Minnesota, called Susie every year on Bobby's birthday. From time to time, he entertained the idea of trying to become Bobby's conservator, but it never progressed beyond talking to Susie.

I wondered why they hadn't kept Bobby at the hospital after the attack, even without his consent. This is called a "5150" in California, referring to the section of the Welfare and Institutions Code which allows an adult to be involuntarily detained for a seventy-two-hour psychiatric hospitalization when they are a danger to themselves or others or are gravely disabled. The hospital felt Bobby didn't meet the criterion of demonstrating a danger to himself or others. Grave disability is defined in California as being unable to provide for food, clothing, or shelter due to a mental disorder. However, psychiatrists will admit that they rarely hospitalize someone for grave disability because California lacks the facilities to care for them. Bobby was considered competent because he could answer basic questions, such as "What is your name?" "What city do you live in?" "Where are you from?" "What is your date of birth?" and "Do you want to stay in the hospital?" This isn't the true definition of competency, but it's been universally accepted as the litmus test.

Interestingly, the American Psychiatric Association's guideline for the psychiatric evaluation of adults includes "failure to care for one-self" as "behavior that prompts urgent action." Specific guidelines for emergency psychiatric evaluation are still lacking. Therefore, the determination whether someone is competent enough to care for themselves or presents a "danger to self" is made by individual clinicians. And because the number of available psychiatric beds in Los Angeles County (and all of California) is miniscule, the threshold of what constitutes a "danger to self," or gravely disabled, continues to rise.

In fact, in 2007, Officer Holloway from the special homeless-oriented team of the Santa Monica Police Department had told me that every morning at 7 a.m., UCLA's Psychiatric Hospital called to let him know their beds were full. And Karen Williams, the Westside Director for L.A. County Mental Health, explained, "In all honesty, we can only consider admission for those in imminent danger to self." Nothing has changed in 2023.

This gives a whole new spin on the debate regarding free will and involuntary treatment. People who qualify for "urgent action" are not getting the treatment they need. We know what the American Psychiatric Association dictates: "failure to care for oneself" requires "urgent action." However, the inability to care for oneself—which may cause eventual danger—is no longer considered worthy of emergency psychiatric care. Only "imminent danger" is worthy of emergency care, such as when someone is holding a gun to their head or threatening to swallow a whole bottle full of deadly medication.

When trying to provide medical care for PEH, free will is considered alongside involuntary treatment. Shouldn't we aim to give the best care possible to someone whose decision-making abilities are gravely limited? Why is our society so reticent about providing care to the sickest among us? How can we pass by, every day, a homeless, one-eyed, filthy man with a watermelon-sized hernia, sitting on a stoop in our neighborhood? Would you let your five-year-old child decide if he or she needed to be hospitalized, or whether to take life-saving medication? The severely mentally ill or demented are often only capable of problem-solving at that developmental level.

We have examples of involuntary psychiatric treatment in movies. Remember "One Flew Over the Cuckoo's Nest," in which Jack Nicholson's character was inappropriately hospitalized and ended up practically comatose as a result? Or the movie "Frances," based on the life of the actor Frances Farmer? She, too, was inappropriately hospitalized by her mother and given seizure-inducing insulin shots in the hopes of "curing" her.

But these types of catastrophic incidents aren't what I'm talking about. This is not how psychiatry is practiced today. We have a broad range of psychiatric medications to treat psychosis and help people lead productive lives. If Bobby were your brother, son, or father, wouldn't you do everything you could to get him help? The debate about free will or whether the gravely disabled fit the criteria for "urgent action" is only the tip of the iceberg. Another problem is the healthcare system that isn't willing to go the extra mile it takes to care for them. Medicare doesn't cover long-term mental health care. Medicaid has extremely strict criteria that makes it exceedingly difficult to provide adequate, long-term care for those with severe mental illness. The state of California hasn't changed their laws for involuntary care for over fifty years, and it has no funding stream for those needing extended, quality care. It's not easy. Care for the severely mentally ill requires many resources and the coordination of many people: outreach workers, social workers, nurses, therapists, lawyers, judges, and medical clinicians. Still, the number of dollars it costs to *not* take care of the mentally ill is even higher. If they lack family assistance, the mentally ill often end up homeless, vulnerable to the risks of the streets or severe physical illness, or they end up in jail, which can exacerbate their symptoms and cost thousands more to take care of them.

At least one-third of the homeless population is mentally ill, according to the Treatment Advocacy Center (2016). They cost the community hundreds of thousands of dollars by over-utilizing our medical and judicial systems. In 2014, The Treatment Advocacy Center cited that 20 percent of the jail population and 15 percent of those in state prisons suffer SMI (severe mental illness)—in total, 356,000 inmates. This is ten times more than the individuals with SMI in state hospitals. A February 2020, a report from California Health Policy Strategies showed the percentage of SMI incarcerated went from 19 percent in 2009 to 31 percent in 2019. *The Gazette* cites that nationwide, jails spend two to three times more on inmates requiring mental health care than they spend on inmates who don't. The Legislative Analyst's Office estimates California's annual cost to incarcerate an inmate at over $81,000.

In addition, as of 2019, the California Hospital Association has experienced a 25 percent drop in the number of inpatient psychiatric beds over the last decade; there are now less than seven thousand beds in total for the entire state of California. Leading mental health experts recommend that across the fifty states, there should be at least fifty public mental health beds per hundred thousand residents to keep up with demand. NAMI (National Alliance on Mental Illness) found that in 2019, L.A. County had only 22.7 such beds per hundred thousand residents. The state of California only has 17.05.

Politicians who don't want to spend money on caring for the severely mentally ill continue to purport the notion that PEH choose to be homeless, and it's within their rights to refuse treatment or resources. Subsequently, the government isn't required to provide the adequate resources many need. Society has clung to the idea that the right to refuse treatment is a precious freedom, even if one qualifies under the APA's guideline for "prompt action." But what about the right to thrive in your community?

Eventually, Bobby was hospitalized against his will. The same psychiatrist who had helped me with William, was also the street psychiatrist. She boldly decided that Bobby's untreated hernia was a "danger to self," especially after Bobby said he couldn't get the surgery because the hernia was filled with animals.

After he was admitted, I went to visit him. His dreads were all cut off, and he was clean and wearing a hospital gown.

"Hey Bobby," I said. "How are you doing? Why are you wearing a hospital gown?" I wanted to see how aware he was of his surroundings.

"I'm okay," he said. "Because I'm in the hospital."

He looked completely different from how I had known him on the street. But I never heard what happened to him after his hospitalization. He wasn't in Santa Monica any longer—hopefully, he was conserved. When someone experiences schizophrenia, the longer they are untreated, the more difficult it is to treat symptoms. Eventually, they will need more and more care. We need to treat people sooner and more aggressively, as if their life depends on it. Because it does!

I asked James O'Connell, MD, former medical director for the Boston Health Care for the Homeless, veteran of working with PEH, and one of my mentors, about the need for more aggressive care for the severely mentally ill. He told me a story about a homeless woman named Mary.

"When I first started doing Street Outreach in Boston, we'd often see a woman who hung out by the steps of city jail. Mary was so paranoid that it took the team about a year to get her to accept a sandwich. She wouldn't accept medical care. One day, she had a psychotic break, which required police intervention. She was hospitalized, put on proper medications, and set up with outpatient treatment. She recovered dramatically and eventually joined the board of Health Care for the Homeless. One day, I ran into her and said, 'Hi Mary, it's so good to see you!' She replied, 'You bastard! You let me sit and rot on those steps for all those years without doing a damn thing!'"

10

THE AMERICAN DREAM?

DURING THE FIRST FEW WEEKS OF STARTING STREET MEDICINE in Santa Monica in January of 2007, I met Michael. He was shy but pleasant, quite overweight, and unkempt as most PEH are, with dirty clothes and a lack of hygiene. He hung out at Reed Park, the same park where I had taken cooking classes at ten years of age. Back then, there weren't any homeless hanging out in Santa Monica. In fact, the first PEH I encountered was during the 1980s, in Malibu. Whenever we drove down Pacific Coast Highway, we would see this man with long straggly hair walking up and down the road. He obviously was mentally ill and at the time, I didn't understand how anyone could be homeless. Around this time, more and more mentally ill started living in the streets due to deinstitutionalization without community follow-up. The stringent Lanterman-Petris-Short (LPS) Act had called for the end of involuntary commitment of people with mental health disorders, and President Reagan made it much more difficult for people to access SSI (federally paid disability).

Michael was one of many PEH I would come to know well, up close and personal. He kept all his belongings on his bicycle, balancing them skillfully in some sort of organized chaos. I approached him at the park and said, "Hey! How are you? Do you need any medical care? Socks? Hygiene kits?" This was (and still is) my standard method of engagement and usually, people will accept something.

With a reserved smile, he said, "No, thank you," and avoided looking at me. The next time I saw him, one of the medical students had managed to engage him. Michael had some sort of rash and had asked for something to treat it. Pleased that my previously spurned efforts were now welcome, I took out an antifungal cream and gave it to him. These small victories feel large; it was as if he had agreed to a life-saving cancer treatment.

When I found Michael the next week, he said the cream hadn't worked, so I arranged for the supervision of his bike and belongings and convinced him to come to the clinic for a proper exam and treatment. He was treated and referred to a dermatologist. But like many PEH, he never went to the appointment with the specialist.

Not many people know much about street medicine, in which healthcare providers go to PEH rather than waiting for them to come to our clinics, offices, and emergency rooms. I'm not sure when the term was first coined, but the practice began in the 1980s when the homeless population began to explode, and primary care physicians realized a good portion of this population was extremely ill. PEH weren't receiving appropriate care. They relied heavily on emergency room care, and they were dying at an alarming rate.

The way street medicine works: a group of outreach workers load up a van and look for PEH under the pier, in the parks and alleys, or on the beach. I walk with my backpack filled with medications and supplies, a clipboard (before the Internet!), and a stethoscope, asking PEH if they needed medical attention. I've taken out sutures, removed staples, cleaned wounds, treated bronchitis and other ailments, and brought patients to the clinic or emergency room.

But why develop the practice of street medicine? Many assume that people living on the streets choose to be homeless, that they choose not to work. "Shouldn't they get their acts together or pull themselves up by their bootstraps?" This common refrain is heard throughout the country. This is America, where anyone can go from "rags to riches" and become a millionaire or even a billionaire. Look at Bill Gates, Oprah, or many other celebrities or professional athletes. This is what our society is all about, the American dream. Anyone and everyone can succeed.

My father took advantage of America's opportunities. He was an aerospace engineer in Iran before immigrating to the US in the 1960s. Here, he earned a master's degree and met my mother, who taught English in Watts. This was her contribution to the world, and I was proud of her for that. When many joined the exodus from Iran after the shah was ousted in 1979, many of our relatives on my father's side came here as well. I was the only member of the family born here and the only one who couldn't speak Farsi. Many of my cousins became doctors and other types of professionals, benefitting from our parents' move to America. We were lucky to have doors opened for us.

According to a 2020 report by the Los Angeles Homeless Services Authority, on any given night in L.A. County, over sixty-six thousand people are unhoused. There aren't enough shelter beds countywide, so more than two-thirds of the homeless population live on the streets. Many are chronically homeless and older than sixty-two years of age.

Also, thousands of children are on the streets living as part of a homeless family. Families and children?! Hm, they might have difficulty reaching their bootstraps. Are these kids getting nutritious meals? Vaccines? Are they going to school? So, the elderly and children are at particular risk, but what about the others? Surely, they can pull themselves up by their bootstraps, get a job, and find someplace to live. Well, 74 percent are disabled. One-third suffer from severe mental health problems, more than 50 percent are depressed, and 35 percent have physical disabilities. Additionally, 42 percent are plagued with addiction. In February 2020, CBS reported that 74 percent of PEH were employed before becoming homeless, and 47 percent have worked within four years of becoming homeless.

And here's a statistic I first learned at a conference: the average age of death for PEH in the U.S. is forty-five! Attendees from around the world voiced similar figures—forty-one in the U.K., forty-seven in Pittsburgh "Well, it's cold in those places," I suggested. "That's why, right?"

Dr. Perri, a street team member from the Boston Health Care for the Homeless Program, explained. He said that a study conducted by Dr. James O'Connell showed the incidence of death in Boston was higher in the summer and fall months than in winter and spring. What do they die of? Heart attack, strokes, cancer, just like the rest of the U.S. population—but thirty years earlier.

A week after his clinic visit, Michael was still not better, so I took things into my own hands. I brought a male outreach worker with me as a chaperone and examined Michael's rash in the men's bathroom at the park. In seconds, I diagnosed him with a severe infection known as balanitis—a swelling and irritation of the glans, or head, of the penis, which almost always indicates diabetes. I measured Michael's blood glucose, and it was 289, extremely high. His blood pressure was elevated to 210/105. He appeared less excited about his diagnosis than I was and declined treatment. But he humored me by listening to my fervent lecture on diabetes and diet.

After a few more park visits, Michael finally agreed to see me at the clinic to receive treatment for his diabetes and hypertension. I declared proudly to anyone who would listen that I had diagnosed diabetes in the field, and now the patient was visiting me in the clinic and doing great.

But then I didn't see him for a while. Months passed. Finally, I found Michael hanging out at another park.

"The cops ran me out of Reed Park," he explained.

"Where've you been?" I asked. "I've been looking for you! Why haven't you come to the clinic? Are you still taking your medications?"

"No," he said, half-smiling and a little embarrassed.

"Do you want to die?" I asked in exasperation. (In retrospect, this is never an effective line of questioning and rarely changes a patient's behavior.)

He shrugged, looking down.

"Okay, you're not going to die any time soon," I said. "But you could get really sick, have a stroke, and then, not be able to walk or talk. You'll need an amputation or dialysis. Life will only become more miserable!"

He shrugged again. His demeanor—head down, shoulders drooping—told me he had given up. Not just on treating his diabetes and hypertension but on everything.

His hopelessness seeped into me until I felt it, too. I had always believed that Michael was chronically depressed, which could have been a major contributing factor to his homelessness. I had also considered the idea that he might have been suffering from slight cognitive disabilities. My goal had been to get him to the clinic, start treating his diabetes and hypertension, develop a relationship of trust with him, and *then* try to address his depression. I should have addressed the depression first.

The figures began to run through my head. The cost of taking care of a stroke victim: approximately $75,000. An amputation could cost $50,000. Dialysis runs as much as $100,000 annually, whereas permanent housing for a year would only be about $15,000.

If a disease emerged, striking hundreds of thousands of people, with a 30 percent five-year mortality rate, the Centers for Disease Control and Prevention would jump to attention and commit enormous resources to curing it. The National Institutes of Health would grant millions of dollars for developing treatments, and the scientist who found the cure would surely be a favorite for the Nobel Prize in Medicine.

A disease like this does exist—homelessness. When someone is homeless, they are in survival mode. *How do I keep my things safe? Where do I get my next meal? Where do I go to the bathroom?* Remember Maslow's hierarchy of needs? When basic needs such as food, water, warmth, and rest aren't met, one's higher needs such as relationships, feelings of accomplishment, and reaching one's full potential will never be realized. Now add to the formula medical needs, drug use, and mental illness. These will rarely be addressed if one's primal needs aren't met.

The beginning of the cure for homelessness is widely available, immediate, and ultimately, cost-saving. Studies show that one person experiencing homelessness can cost a community hundreds of thousands of dollars a year in medical and legal expenses. So, what can be done? Assertive mental health programs for PEH increase opportunities for housing and improve their quality of life. Focusing attention on the high-risk PEH—those with mental illnesses, substance abuse problems and certain, chronic medical conditions—will likely decrease mortality rates. But first and most important, the homeless need housing. That's what we should have prioritized with Michael, followed closely with addressing his mental health issues.

Despite some obvious approaches, homelessness still exists in epidemic proportions. Why? Some PEH have serious, untreated medical conditions that worsen and perpetuate their inability to work. The severely mentally ill PEH are not being placed in long-term psychiatric care because there are simply not enough care centers available, and they are not being placed in enriched case facilities (a place to live that provides not only medications, housing and meals, but also a therapeutic environment with things like art or gardening) where they can best recover and thrive. Many have severe substance use disorders. Being on the streets is usually their rock bottom and they can't dig themselves out.

Even worse, often they are demonized instead of treated for their drug use. Our society stigmatizes drug users, especially in shelters or hospitals. They are told they deserve whatever they've done to their bodies. Sometimes, adequate pain relief is withheld. And so, they leave the hospital. Many have died because their opiate use wasn't treated in the hospital while they were being treated for another serious medical condition. Their mental health issues often aren't considered, as providers believe "it's just their drug or alcohol use" causing the problem. Routinely, the medical establishment gives up on them. They're thrown in jail for drug possession, worsening their chances of succeeding in society. Most shelters won't allow drug use, so those with drug use issues find it impossible to stay. We need to provide compassionate, respectful, quality care to this very vulnerable group. We need to be a "good" community.

A good doctor doesn't judge their patients and sees them for what they are—fellow humans with emotions, thoughts, likes, dislikes, and opinions. When Steve, my early mentor in Mexico, joked with his patients to put them at ease, or when I went out of my way to make sure the surgery patient had morphine before his painful exams, or when Dr. Castro tried to understand a family's culture and respect it, or when an outreach worker buys someone a pack of cigarettes to encourage them to get treated at the hospital—all of us are, I hope, just trying to treat others how we'd like to be treated. One of my residents paid for an Uber to make sure a patient could get to an appointment. That's being a good doctor! Another colleague drove a patient to her home an hour away because she didn't have bus money. Good doctor! My volunteer always offers her hand for patients to hold during procedures. Good, soon-to-be doctor! One of my residents told me that when his patient asked to pray with him, he "meditated" instead because he isn't religious. Good doctor. Another colleague created a locker system for our homeless patients who kept losing their medications. Good doctor!

Months later, Michael told one of the outreach workers he wanted me to check his blood sugar the next time I went out to the park. I found him, and his blood glucose was still high, 321. He agreed to take a ride to the clinic for refills of his medications, and he accepted an outreach worker's invitation to stay at the local shelter, where his bicycle and possessions would be stored safely. It was a good first step.

We know the cure, so why is it not widely implemented? Why is homelessness untreated? I keep returning to our cultural values. It's time to redefine the American Dream. There's nothing wrong with wanting to succeed, improve the opportunities available to your family, or even become rich. But what if this wasn't the main focus in our lives? What if we tried to make a difference in the lives of other people, too? What if we gave something to those who need it most, even if they're strangers, even if they use drugs or alcohol, and even if they're severely mentally ill and living on the streets? What if that was the American Dream? What if we could all be good doctors, good people, a good community? What if that was the American Dream?

Addendum: In the last decade, many counties have taken on a housing-first model in "treating" PEH, especially if they are frequent flyers to the hospitals and the emergency room. For example, when Covid-19 hit, California started housing the more fragile PEH in hotels, which is a great start. However, with the severely mentally ill, we are learning that treatment first—such as with long-acting, injectable antipsychotics, either on the streets or during hospitalization—is usually needed before they can accept housing.

11

DANIEL'S STORY

"I HATE THE PERSON I'VE BECOME. I'M FORCED TO BE MEAN and uncaring." Daniel's head was down, and tears welled in his eyes. He had these amazing powder-blue eyes, which always seemed so striking against the smudged dirt on his face.

"What do you mean?" I looked at him. This was out of character, this emotion and despair.

"This is not who I am. But this is what the streets do to you. They turn you into evil, a loner. Not caring about anyone."

"I know you got jumped last week, Daniel," I said. "Is that what's bothering you?"

He shrugged. His eyes were empty.

"I used to play the guitar professionally," he said. "I was in a band. I had a life, Doc."

I heard his Kentucky drawl then, like syrup when he strung more than a few words together. Which hadn't happened before today. I started seeing Daniel in June of 2005, just a few months after starting work at the Needle Exchange. He was tall and his long gray hair was perpetually greasy. He wore a stringy, unkempt beard. He was very thin, with hollow cheeks. In my notes, I described him as, "disheveled, dirty and lethargic," which could have described any number of my patients at the clinic. Daniel often had food or vomit in his beard, and he came to the clinic smelling like urine. I had seen feces on his pants many times. He looked like the typical older, severely psychotic homeless man often seen in the homeless hot spots of Los Angeles, digging through the trash and talking to himself.

As I listened to Daniel talk, a realization struck me like a thunderbolt. *He's not schizophrenic or delusional! He's severely depressed with psychotic features.* This was easier to treat because patients still had their ability to reason intact. He was using heroin to treat his depression. I see this quite often. Many of the drug users I see are self-treating a mental illness, chronic pain condition, or both.

I straightened up and looked again into his vivid eyes. "Daniel, you seem very depressed. I can refer you to the Downtown Mental Health Clinic. Medications might help so you wouldn't need drugs."

"Ok, Doc." His head stayed down when he gave his passive agreement. He didn't seem to have much hope that anything could change for him and with the circumstances of his life, I guess I couldn't blame him. I, however, was excited. I was certain that if we could treat his mental illness, he could get clean and start his life again. This was a naïve thought. Over time, I'd learn that the reality of surviving Skid Row wasn't that easy.

Los Angeles has the highest number of PEH in the nation, with the highest concentration in the Skid Row area. Heroin (and now, Fentanyl) users are at a higher risk of death, because overdose is a common and often deadly consequence. Daniel also had hepatitis C, as about 80 percent of injection drug users do. Thus, the trifecta of chronic medical illness, mental illness, and substance use leads to the highest risk of death.

Daniel normally slept in a park or under a bridge. For a meager income, he washed car windows with newspapers and a spray bottle of mostly water. He came to the Needle Exchange almost daily and attended the group sessions. The groups were a way for users to have community, learn skills, and avoid judgment for who they were and what they did. I saw Daniel regularly, mostly for scabies, an infestation of the skin by microscopic mites. In fact, I had seen him about ten times for various skin conditions and had already tried to refer him to Homeless Health Care's outpatient drug treatment before the day he opened up to me. He hadn't gone.

I gave him the referral to Downtown Mental Health. He didn't go. Later, I referred him to another outpatient treatment program. He didn't go. A few months passed. I picked up some Seroquel (a medication for both depression and psychosis) samples from our main office, gave them to Daniel, and he said he would try them. *Whew! I felt a glimmer of hope. Finally, I had made progress.* Then I didn't see him for two months.

He came into the clinic again, this time with a leg infection. Nothing else seemed to have changed. He was lethargic, resigned, downbeat.

He watched as I worked on his leg. "Got picked up," he said.

I knew he meant jail. "How long?"

"Three days."

Nodding, I continued working. Classic rock played through the small speaker nearby. We had this in common, and we'd often talk about rock groups we liked from the seventies. He told me he had once played in sessions for groups like Pure Prairie League. As he spoke about his past life in music, his eyes flickered with life. If you look hard enough, even at people who try to hide it, you can see their specialness, uniqueness, and humanity.

"I was thinking about ending it all, Doc. On my birthday."

Shit. "When was your birthday?"

"Couple days ago."

"Did the medicine I gave you a while back help?"

"I don't know." He gazed into the distance, his blue eyes cloudy and dull again.

Before he left, I gave him some more Seroquel and asked him to please try it. I didn't see him until three months later. He limped into the clinic, holding his upper arm.

"Got hit by a car, Doc. I think it's broke."

"Okay," I said. "I'm sending you to the clinic down the street. I can order x-rays there for my patients."

He shook his head. "No offense, Doc, but it ain't gonna happen." He knew well the difficulties of getting medical care without insurance in those days.

We went back and forth about it for a while. I decided to walk him to the clinic to make sure he got his X-ray done. Despite a potentially broken arm, he was more animated than usual and seemed glad for the company, even if just to walk down the street. On the way to the clinic, he introduced me to his "godfather."

"Doc, this is Skipper. Skip, this is the Doc I was tellin' you about." Skipper was a bald white guy, in his fifties or sixties, wearing a blue windbreaker. He didn't seem too excited to meet me, barely acknowledging us.

As we continued walking, Daniel leaned toward me and lowered his voice. "He's the only one I trust out here. And, of course, you."

At the other clinic, they wouldn't let me order an X-ray for Daniel. He looked at me with a "told ya so" look. I told him to go to the ER, but he never went. Someone using opiates can't risk a long wait or hospitalization. So, like many, he went undiagnosed and untreated.

That was in January of 2007. For the remainder of the year, I saw Daniel a few times—for more skin infections, an eye infection, cracked ribs, scabies, etc. One day, fed up with his recurrence of scabies, instead of handing him a tube of cream, my assistant Patty and I undressed him, donned our gloves, and slathered the cream all over his body. We threw away his old clothes and gave him new clothes to wear, and another set to change into after washing off the cream in twelve hours. But it didn't matter if he washed the cream off or not. Slathering him with the anti-scabies medication would kill the mites. But scabies is difficult to treat because anything made of cloth must be washed—pillows, backpack, sleeping bag. While living on the streets, Daniel didn't have the ability to do that and so, he kept coming back with scabies.

After we'd covered him with the cream, Patty commented, "He looks like a wet puppy." Daniel chuckled faintly at this. He was skin and bones, his wet hair matted against his head. His beard was equally matted and dirty. That visit, I didn't try to refer him anywhere, and I didn't give him more anti-depressants. I'm not sure why. Maybe I had become resigned, too.

Then, in April of 2008, he came to me complaining about a groin hernia he'd had for some time. But it was getting larger, and he had been vomiting. He had gone to LAC/USC (Los Angeles County USC hospital), where they had kept him for six days. But then he was discharged without surgery.

At that time, a new program had begun. The Full-Service Program was established through a grant from L.A. County's Department of Mental Health. The program assigned mentally ill and homeless patients, if they qualified, to a case manager who would hook them up with psychiatry, a medical home, drug treatment, and HOUSING. Full-Service Partnership! I signed him up, and he qualified! He was assigned a case worker, Pearlina, who soon informed me he wasn't making his appointments.

Meanwhile, Daniel had increased his heroin use to deal with the pain from his hernia. He had been back to LA/USC twice, and to Harbor-UCLA once. Because his heart rate was in the forties, they had said he would need medical clearance before they could operate. It has been my experience that when some chronic opiate users are withdrawing, their heart rate becomes low. I gave him a prescription for pain medicine, hoping to decrease his need for heroin, and recommended he try Cedars Sinai for surgery. He didn't fill the prescription and didn't go to Cedars. He continued to miss appointments with Pearlina. One day, I called her myself. With some coaxing, she agreed to meet him at the Needle Exchange. I spoke to James, the director, who agreed to call her the next time Daniel showed up. Meanwhile, I made a pre-op clinic appointment for Daniel at LAC/USC and gave him another prescription for pain medicine.

Finally, Daniel met Pearlina at the Needle Exchange. James was now on board. He was working closely with Pearlina, trying to get Daniel's birth certificate from Kentucky in order to attain proper ID for housing. I kept trying to schedule psychiatry appointments, which he never kept. He also missed his pre-op appointment. I tried to schedule an appointment with surgery, but they wouldn't see him until he did the pre-op. Daniel told me he couldn't find a pharmacy that carried the pain medicine I'd prescribed. I made another pre-op appointment for him at LAC/USC. Pearlina found a sober living place, but Daniel left after one day, saying he didn't like it.

Over the next couple of months, Daniel never did fill the prescription, but James took him to the DMV to get his ID and started addressing his legal issues. He also hooked him up with a methadone clinic. Methadone is used as a pain reliever but also for opiate replacement or detoxification to avoid withdrawal symptoms. But Daniel missed his appointment because he was arrested. James rescheduled the methadone clinic appointment. Eventually, Daniel went to the clinic but soon started missing appointments there, too. Are you frustrated yet? Do you see how dealing with "the homeless situation" isn't cut and dry? It's not that Daniel didn't want to make his appointments but when you are experiencing homelessness and use heroin, your priorities are all about survival. This includes making sure you have adequate heroin, which, at any point, can land you in jail.

I saw Daniel in December. His hernia had grown to the size of a mango, and I decided to take matters into my own hands. He couldn't stop heroin because of the pain from his hernia. He couldn't get clean from heroin without being housed. I spoke to my department's inpatient director at Harbor-UCLA to see about hospitalizing Daniel to pre-op him. She agreed. I then called a surgery-attending colleague of mine there to see if he'd be willing to operate on Daniel on a scheduled date if the Family Medicine team did the pre-op, exam, and studies while he was in the hospital. He agreed! At the same time, Pearlina found Daniel housing at the Weingart hotel in the Skid Row area, and James convinced the methadone clinic to hold Daniel's spot while he was in the hospital. I requested that the family medicine team provide Daniel with Methadone while he was hospitalized. Pearlina asked the Weingart hotel to hold his spot until his release from the hospital. All was agreed upon.

James drove Daniel to the hospital on February 3, 2009. He had his surgery on February 9 and was released on the 17th. His room wasn't available, so Homeless Health Care provided emergency housing at another hotel. Daniel told James he wanted to go to detox, followed by a ninety-day program. He went to detox on March 11, followed by a ninety-day residential program. He started seeing a psychiatrist at Downtown Mental Health and was prescribed medications that this time, he took.

I saw Daniel a couple of months later. His hair was clean, shiny, and cut to shoulder-length. His beard was nicely trimmed as well, and he had gained about forty pounds. Best of all, he had life in his powder-blue eyes.

Studies show that housing the homeless cuts death rates by up to 500 percent and "assertive community treatment for the severely mentally ill," which includes housing, results in a 62 percent reduction in symptoms. In fact, the most cost-effective and successful treatment for the mentally ill PEH is housing and "assertive community" plans like the Full-Service Partnership Program. In Daniel's case, none of my attempts to offer resources came to fruition until he was met at his usual hangout and driven somewhere, and a team of physicians coordinated to work around his individual needs. Many studies conclude that housing PEH saves communities millions of dollars from legal issues (e.g., jail) and emergency medical care alone. A 2021 study showed that emergency room use by PEH is three times the U.S. norm and has increased 80 percent over the past decade. Also, PEH are more likely to be frequent users (four or more visits a year) or super users (twenty or more visits). One study in Boston followed the lives of one hundred and nineteen PEH over seven years and discovered that these individuals had made over eighteen thousand emergency room visits.

The city and county of Los Angeles have learned that housing PEH and providing wrap-around services where needed is the most cost-effective approach for the community. In fact, L.A. County voters approved Measure H in 2017, which increased sales tax to provide an ongoing revenue stream for these services, an estimated $355 million per year for ten years. But we're still not out of the woods. Creating new housing is costly, and we need to come up with creative ways to house people. For example, putting thousands of people experiencing homelessness into hotels during the Covid-19 pandemic was brilliant, a good example of thinking outside the box. Furthermore, as we saw with Daniel, it takes a lot of energy and resources to work with one disabled individual, especially when drug use and mental illness are involved. Finally, we have statistics that show housing first is not only the moral answer to homelessness, but the most cost-effective approach, too. Keep doing the right thing, Los Angeles, by providing programs so that more people like Daniel receive a second chance at life.

A worker from Homeless Health Care worked with Pearlina to find Daniel a sober living house in San Pedro after his ninety-day program. The last I'd heard, he was still housed, clean, and sober.

With my dad on my fourth birthday.

My siblings: Michelle (top) at sixteen, me at eleven, Gerry at twenty-three. At my house in Brentwood.

Weekly dinners with Grandma, Grandpa, and various relatives. Mom and Dad in picture, too.

My high school graduation; mom wanted to wear her master's gown.

"El Dumpay"

The clinic in "El Dumpay,"
age nineteen, 1986.

College graduation lunch
with Mom and Dad.

College graduation day w Mom,
Dad, Grandma and Grandpa.

Visiting a patient on the Navajo reservation outside Winslow, Arizona as a fourth-year medical student in 1993.

Graduation from medical school.

My mom and I in 2006, before she was diagnosed with dementia.

Homeless Health Care LA's Center for Harm Reduction aka the Needle Exchange, in Skid Row. Began working for them October 2004.

Me and nurse practitioner Jen King from HHCLA working on a wound in the streets.

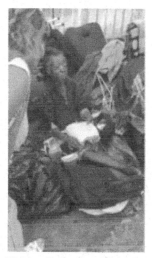

Visiting Barbara in Skid Row. She had severe dementia and was eventually housed in a board and care.

Doing outreach at the beginning of the pandemic.

Advocating for expanding the definition of grave disability.

Left to right: Sarah Dusseault (boardmember, Los Angeles Homeless Services Authority (LAHSA), Brittany Weissman (Executive Director, National Alliance on Mental Illness (NAMI), Katherine Barger (LA County Supervisor), Anthony Ruffin (LA County Department of Mental Health outreach), me, Emily DeFraites (Section Chief, LA Veterans Affairs Healthcare System)

This is "Patty" at the last hotel before hospitalization.

Me with Marcia Gay Harden as Doctor P on the set of *Tell It Like a Woman.*

Administering a long-acting, injectable antipsychotic medication to a person experiencing homelessness.

12

COOKIE

I WANT TO SHARE A STORY WITH YOU ABOUT A LOVEABLE little terrier mix named Cookie. She was a small white dog with a fluff of longer fur around her face. Her dad had her dressed in a pink sweater. I met her in November 2012, at Homeless Health Care's Harm Reduction Center (aka the Needle Exchange). One of our clients brought her in and introduced her. She was about three months old and as soon as I saw her eyes, I fell in love. She wasn't in typical puppy mode—lots of energy and exploring everything in sight or smell range—and this worried me. Her dad, a homeless heroin user, assured us he was taking good care of her. I told him to come in any time with any questions or problems and someone would call me.

A couple of weeks later, Dyhan, a colleague, called me because Cookie wasn't eating, and her dad was worried. Unfortunately, I didn't receive the message until the next day, which was Thanksgiving. I felt terribly about missing the call and prayed she would be all right. Dyhan and I imagined the worst. In two weeks, her dad brought Cookie in again. She was doing great. I convinced him to let me take Cookie in for a check-up and her first set of shots.

He brought her the next week. While I continued to see patients, a coworker babysat the puppy. Then, I took her home. She was wearing a little pink sweater, and I imagined it was her first car ride. She stood up on her hind legs, looking outside. On high alert, she seemed fascinated by everything she saw. She jumped up to the front seat with me, placed her front paws on the dashboard, balancing her body so she could look through the front window. After some time, she curled up on the seat and fell asleep.

As soon as we arrived home, I gave her a bath. I filled a bowl with the food my other dogs eat, and she inhaled it. Around the house, she explored everything and wanted to play with everyone. Daisy, my fifty-five-pound basset/beagle mix, was her new BFF. They ran around the house non-stop, playing with each other and napping in between. I took her on a hike, and she followed Molly, my six-year-old Jack-Russell/shih tzu/Maltese mix, off her leash the entire time. She was a natural!

Cookie slept in bed with me and the other three, curled up in the nook of my neck. That first night, I cried, dreading already the moment I'd have to give her back. It had been so cold outside, and I couldn't imagine sending her back out on the streets. But I had given my word that I would return her.

As promised, I took her for a check-up and vaccines, and I made an ID tag for her with my name and phone number, just in case. The following week, I drove her back to the Needle Exchange. During the ride, she curled up on the seat again, sleeping the whole way. I couldn't help but think it might be the last time I'd see her. At the clinic, her dad greeted her with a new outfit, a fuchsia and black striped leotard. He picked her up, and she licked his face with glee. As they walked out, Cookie wagged her tail, excited to be back with her dad.

———

A few weeks went by. I couldn't stop thinking about her. My coworkers knew I had struggled with giving her back. I felt like the universe wanted me to have her. Then, on Thursday, January 10, 2013, when I came into the clinic, I asked Dyhan if Cookie's dad had been in.

"Yes," she said. "He came in yesterday and said he'd stop by again today."

I started my day. While opening an abscess on a regular patient, my phone rang.

"Dr. Partovi! Cookie was hit by a car. She can't walk." He had used the number on her ID tag. He was twenty blocks away.

"Bring her here." My heart was pounding as I worked on my next patient. I could barely concentrate and fought to keep it together. As I moved from patient to patient, I kept an eye on the door.

"She's here," Dyhan finally announced.

I went out to the waiting room. Cookie was lying on her dad's jacket on the table, her back legs splayed out. She wasn't moving but she was awake.

"I'm taking her to the veterinary ER," I said.

He nodded, looking scared. "Do what you have to do for her," he said.

In the other room, a patient with a large abscess was moaning. I hurried to treat him, yelling that I needed help. An assistant came in and I told her what to do as I numbed the patient and began to open him up. I could barely concentrate. I wanted to get back to Cookie. Ten minutes later, I let my assistant, Angelica, finish up and carefully transferred Cookie to my car.

As I drove to the hospital, I thought about the last time she'd been in my car, sleeping in the seat. Comfortable and safe with me.

During the journey, I watched her, and she watched me. I hoped she recognized me and was comforted, but I couldn't be sure. At one point on the 10 West, I thought she had stopped breathing. Her eyes turned opaque and stayed open. I yelled, "Cookie, live!" I said this repeatedly, starting chest compressions with my right hand as I drove with the left. She came back to me, looking up with an expression that seemed to say "What?"

After that, I wouldn't let her sleep. As I continued to push on her ribs (not sure what the hell I was doing), I directed her again and again to keep living. After the longest car ride of my life, I carried her into the trusted pet hospital, where I have been multiple times with my other kids. By then, I was sobbing, barely able to relay her story at the desk.

They took her back right away. The young ER doc came out fifteen minutes later and was compassionate and patient with me. Every time she came out, I'd ask immediately if Cookie was still alive. And she was. She had a crushed pelvis, femur, and tail, and a severed spinal cord—resulting in no anal tone. They were giving her fluids and IV pain medication.

They warned me that Cookie wouldn't walk again, and she would be incontinent. I didn't care. "Just keep her alive," I pleaded. They gave her a blood transfusion, and she survived the night. Her blood pressure and blood count were stable.

I saw her the next morning. It was hard. Her eyes were sad. I kissed her and told her I loved her. The doctor said she would need at least two surgeries to fix her pelvis and femur. I immediately planned to keep her and take care of her complicated needs.

I was distraught with guilt. I thought about one of my friends, who had been upset when I gave Cookie back to her dad. "Dogs belonging to the homeless never look happy," she had said. And I had tried to explain to her that I see many dogs with our homeless patients. These dogs have many of the same gifts housed dogs have. The owner has someone to love and be loved by. Sometimes dogs give them purpose; there's a healing power in being accepted by another living being, no matter what. Yet, one may ask, "If PEH can't take care of themselves, how can they take care of an animal?" Studies show that animals help humans heal physically and emotionally, but the dog of a PEH is at greater risk, especially in urban areas. They are at risk of malnutrition, a lack of medical care, including getting neutered and vaccinated, theft, abandonment and of course, getting hit by a car. Is the risk worth it? Many PEH are mentally competent with good judgement; thus, a blanket statement doesn't seem fair. We know that when it comes to ameliorating a homeless person's physical and mental health and substance abuse, the best strategy is to house them, and it's also the most cost-effective strategy. Consequently, I would think the best way to care for animals belonging to PEH is to house their caretakers.

On the second day, the surgeon was hesitant to operate on Cookie. The dog had too many injuries, he said. He didn't understand my persistence. He kept repeating the "facts": she wouldn't be able to walk, and she'd be incontinent.

So, strap those wheels on her back legs and throw some diapers on her. I couldn't understand his hesitance. *Don't dogs get hit by cars all the time?*

From the first moment I saw her lying in the clinic, I had wanted Cookie to live. I didn't think I was being aggressive with her care, but merely doing what anyone would do. At one point, the surgeon said, "I have to question your motives." I called the first vet, Dr. Caigney, in tears. She soothed me, claiming the surgeon merely wanted to make sure I knew the extent of her wounds.

The next day, I saw Cookie in the ICU after surgery. She'd had another transfusion and a central line was placed in her neck for IV fluids, medications, and drawing blood. She had a nasogastric tube for her feeds, a catheter for her urine, and an IV line in her front paw for continuous pain medicine.

They had operated on her left femur and pelvis, and she was standing on her forepaws when I walked in. One of the vet techs said she was being "feisty." *That's my girl!* I stayed with Cookie for a while. She was having a tough time getting comfortable, so I propped her head with a Spiderman blanket and petted her gently until she fell asleep.

During this time, I experienced a roller coaster of emotions. Her feistiness encouraged me and yet, guilt and despair tugged at my heart. I had been taking a series of personal growth seminars with Landmark and in the most recent one, we learned that empowerment can be a choice made in moments of despair. To choose empowerment, you need to have something in front of you, like a goal, and you need to be in action. Thinking about that lesson on a Saturday morning, I decided Cookie was not only going to live but also thrive and inspire others. She could be a service dog with handicapped kids, an encouragement to anyone who crossed her future path. And with that goal, I went into action. First, finances. I asked for help from the veterinary hospital, and they gave me a 5 percent professional discount. I made some calls to inquire about refinancing my house and asked my boss at Homeless Health Care to increase my hours. He complied by almost doubling my hours. I also sent in an application to work at Harbor's Urgent Care and took extra shifts at other facilities.

I visited Cookie at the hospital every day. I got to know the receptionists, the vet techs, and the doctors. One of the techs told me the story of a dog who looked like Cookie and had also been struck by a car. The owner hadn't been able to pay for her care, so the tech had paid and fostered her, like I was doing for Cookie. Her story was extremely encouraging. When I mentioned the surgeon who hadn't been very positive, she told me he had come in on Sunday, his day off, to check on Cookie. He was back in my good graces! Cookie had touched him, too. In fact, she was a rock star at the hospital. Everyone knew about her and would comment about her progress and how amazing she was.

My regular veterinarian, Dr. Hernandez, called me. Coincidentally, her dog, Pickles, was also in the hospital at that time, in the cage right under Cookie's! She had heard about Cookie's accident and remembered her from when I'd brought her for a check-up and shots. During our phone call, she was incredibly supportive. She said she was proud of me for being so aggressive on Cookie's behalf and told me about another dog she had, Scooter, who was a paraplegic and used a cart to "scoot" around. Scooter was a happy dog and loved his life, she said, and she knew Cookie would follow suit. Dr. Hernandez's support was touching and very comforting.

They decided to amputate Cookie's right leg and tail because she had lost feeling in both. Animals often self-mutilate limbs without feeling, which opens a risk for infections. Ironically, Cookie's dad came that same day with a bad infection on his right leg. As I worked on his leg, Cookie's right leg was being amputated. I brought him up to date with Cookie's recovery, and he was grateful she was alive and doing well.

Ten days later, I brought her home and that first week, we visited the vet every single day for one thing or another. She developed an abscess at the amputation site, which required another surgery. She chewed off her catheter (yes, even with the cone of shame on!), and they performed a procedure to enter the bladder and fish it out. I had my own tasks to do. I learned how to squeeze her bladder to get urine out; she couldn't do it by herself. At first, this was daunting, but I got used to it. I would squeeze her about three times a day. She had no control of her bowels, so I bought Costco brand newborn diapers. They worked great but because she was missing a leg, they kept falling off. I found a way to keep them on by using a safety pin and attaching the diaper to her fuchsia fuzzy vest! Her butt was a bit raw, so I used diaper cream, too. Cookie would wiggle whenever I tried to put her diapers on, just like a baby. She slept in bed with the rest of the gang, often putting her head in the nook of my neck. So cute! Unless the diaper fell off during the night, then it was less cute! She was eating and drinking well.

Often, I brought her to the Needle Exchange with me, and she got lots of attention. She'd hang out with me in the little procedure room, mostly sleeping but still doing her magic by being so cute. Her dad hadn't seen her yet. Dyhan and I thought he was avoiding her, which was understandable. He probably felt some guilt, too. I bought Cookie a new stroller and took her everywhere in it. At home, we'd jog with the other dogs as I pushed her in it. She would sit up, watching all the exciting things happening around her. She loved it! I even took her hiking on our usual trail. Pushing the stroller added to the workout for me, but it was worth it. On the trail, she looked around, barked as dogs came by, and licked everyone who stopped to pet her.

But the most exciting thing that happened was also quite unexpected. Within a few days of getting out of the hospital, Cookie started walking on her own! One day, I placed her on the couch while I went out to the front yard. The next thing I knew, she was on the living room floor, walking towards the door to see what I was doing. After that, I couldn't keep her still. She'd follow me wherever I went, wiggling her little body while walking on her front legs. She even figured how to get down the few stairs leading to the front and back yard. She couldn't get *up* the stairs and she still wasn't really using the remaining back leg yet. She walked using only her forelegs while her back leg stuck out and dragged at a ninety-degree angle. It reminded me of a gymnastic move on the vault—amazing and adorable!

Our routine became: squeeze out pee, clean bottom, change diapers, safety pin to vest (while dealing with the smell as best as possible!), take her daily in the stroller. When we jogged to the beach, I would let her roam on the grass to practice her two-legged wiggle.

One morning, about a month after coming home from the hospital, I opened her diaper, and it was empty. I put her in the backyard and watched to see what she would do. Right away, she started doing what I call "the poop dance." Circling and squeezing, circling and squeezing, for what felt like hours but was likely a couple minutes while I recorded with my phone, until—success! She pooped! I was so excited; I posted the video on YouTube! So many people were rooting for Cookie. Later that same day at the beach, she peed on her own. Two miracles in one day! I emailed my vet, "Guess who has anal tone?!" After that day, Cookie started using her back leg and within a week, she was walking, peeing, and pooping.

Now Cookie runs with all of us, hikes off leash—often leading the pack, goes up and down stairs and plays with her BFF, Daisy, regularly. On the day I took her home from the hospital, the surgeon told me he'd never met anyone like me, and he was happy I had stepped up to take care of her (and her bills). "Most people can't or won't take care of animals after a severe trauma," he said. Wouldn't it be great if there were more like me? What if, like humans, we save the animals without thinking about the cost of the veterinary bill or the extra effort to care for them? What if we take care of everyone because we are all connected? When some of us thrive, others thrive more. It's like electricity, the connections. Caring for Cookie and her dad the way I do radiates positivity toward those they encounter.

I'm so proud of Cookie, and so encouraged by her strength and will to live—not only live but thrive! She truly is a miracle girl and to me, a gift of love I never could have anticipated. I'm excited for what the future holds for both of us and in every way, she has been the inspiration I envisioned.

Addendum: Cookie was my heartmate for almost eight years! Saving her was one of the best choices I ever made. She passed suddenly in November of 2020, while I was on vacation. My heart has been broken ever since. Saving her was one of the best choices I ever made.

13

MISSING PARIS

I WAS GETTING READY TO GO TO THE NEEDLE EXCHANGE ON A Tuesday morning when I received a phone call.

"Dr. Partovi, this is Laurie from Portals Mental Health. I'm calling to let you know that Paris Crawford passed away last week."

It wasn't a good connection. There was static and background noise, and it took me a few seconds to understand what she was saying. Once I understood, it stopped me dead in the tracks of my morning rush. I sat down, hands on my head, and began to cry. I was getting tired of those calls.

Paris (this is the name he gave us) had come to the clinic for the first time because of cold symptoms. He was also hoping to attain housing. I noticed his blood pressure was elevated and my assistant wrote "irregular" heart rate on his chart.

A sixty-four-year-old, Black man, Paris was originally from Ohio but had been living on the streets of L.A. He had a flamboyant style of dress and he'd recently been released from prison. The first time we met, Paris wore a huge, silver Star of David supported by many, multi-colored beads, and bright pink Ugg boots. On other occasions,

I'd see him in a white parka vest with a white faux-fur collar. He wore that by itself, without a shirt underneath, and—of course, the pink Ugg boots. I appreciated his flair for fashion. I, too, liked pink, and statement pieces, and boots. I've always loved fashion.

As a teen, I'd sometimes borrow clothing or accessories from friends to make outfits work. Living in Brentwood, I had to keep up with the well-off kids. Both of my parents had grown up quite poor. None of my grandparents had received much education. Mom grew up on welfare and Dad's father was a shoemaker and his mom a homemaker with six kids! My dad grew up in a small village in Iran. My dad became educated and worked as an engineer and, after immigrating to America, was able to buy a small house in Brentwood, which, in the 1970s, was an upper middle-class neighborhood of West Los Angeles. My parents didn't appreciate the need for expensive clothes. "I'm not made of money," they would both say—something they had in common! Mostly, we shopped at Fedco (which was like K-mart but for government employees) for everything, including my clothes. It was humiliating. When I was ten years old, I started cleaning my neighbor's house for ten dollars a week so I could buy my own clothes.

So, I appreciated Paris's efforts to look good, especially with limited resources. Whenever I complimented his taste, he said simply, with a hint of a smile, "I like pink." Paris was diagnosed with schizophrenia. He never told me much about his past.

That first visit, I tried to focus on his symptoms. "Do you have high blood pressure?" I asked.

"That's what they've told me for the last twenty years." His face showed nothing—no surprise, worry, or anything else.

"Do you ever get chest pain or shortness of breath?"

"Sometimes, on and off." Again, he didn't seem concerned.

I gave him a referral to one of the primary care clinics in Skid Row so he could get treatment and regular monitoring for hypertension and its potential side effects. I explained the risks of untreated hypertension: stroke, heart attack, and kidney failure. He continued looking at me impassively. Not sure he was understanding the urgency of what I was telling him, I said, "I've seen people with these problems, and I don't want you to suffer from them. Also, I'm going to hook you up with the Full-Service Partnership Program to help you with housing and get you back on your psychiatric medications."

He lit up. "I'd love housing!"

Finally, a response! He wanted housing, that was all.

Over the following months, he continued returning to the clinic for assorted reasons, including the hepatitis vaccines we supplied to our clients. The next time I saw him, a few months later, I asked, "Did you go to the clinic yet?"

"No, I don't like to take medicines," he told me. He never offered any rationalization. But he had followed up with Portals Mental Health for the Full-Service Partnership Program (FSP), and they'd been able to find him housing. FSP is a mental health program specifically for PEH who are willing to accept resources. They provide "wrap-around" services and housing.

I reminded him again of the potential problems related to untreated hypertension. I told him I was really worried about him.

He looked up at me and added a little inflection to his voice, as if to please me. "Ok, I'll take the medicines."

Two miracles in one day!

A few weeks after that, Paris signed up for a same day appointment with me. I hadn't spoken to him for a while, but I'd see him, hanging out in the lobby of the clinic, sitting by himself in a corner. I'd ask him whether he was still in his apartment, and he always said yes.

When he showed up for the appointment, he looked thinner, possibly ill. He wasn't wearing his usual garb, just a regular shirt and pants.

"What's going on, Paris?"

"Well, I've been feeling short of breath, especially when I walk. Do you have any medicine for this?"

"Chest pain?"

"Just a little tightness."

I looked at his chart. He'd recently been hospitalized for the same thing.

"They told me I have a blockage in one of the vessels in my heart."

I looked up, impressed with his understanding.

"But I left after two days," he said. "I don't like hospitals."

I continued to ask him questions and discovered he wasn't taking any of his medications. Whenever he answered, I noticed he had difficulty speaking in full sentences. He had to stop to catch his breath. I took his pulse, and his heart rate was fast. Choosing my words carefully, I told him I thought he was experiencing heart failure. When an artery is blocked, I explained, part of the heart can die and thus, the organ no longer pumps very effectively. He said he understood. I gave him aspirin to chew and nitroglycerin for chest pain.

"You need to go to the hospital," I said. "I'd like to call the paramedics to take you. If they come, will you go with them?"

He straightened up and said softly, "No."

I had learned the hard way, paramedics wouldn't take people against their will, even if they are obviously mentally impaired and not making rational decisions about their health. I tried another tactic. "Do you understand how serious this is? I rarely recommend that people go straight to the ER from the clinic. So, if I do, I really mean it!"

He nodded with the calm but exasperating look he had. "I understand. But I'm not going to the hospital."

"What if I drove you to the hospital? Would you go then?"

"I'm not going to the hospital." He stood up as though ready to leave. "Anyway, I feel much better with the medicine you gave me."

Great, that proves further that you're in heart failure. I tried to convince him one more time, then gave him prescriptions for aspirin, a medicine to lower his blood pressure and heart rate, and nitroglyc-erin. After I handed the papers to him, I said, "I'll be here next Tuesday. Will you come?"

"I'll be here."

That was the last time I'd seen him and of course, he hadn't shown up for that appointment. And now he was gone.

"Susan, are you there?" Laurie was still on the line, waiting for my response.

"I'm still here," I said.

She explained that Paris had not kept his appointments to see the psychiatrist, either. He hadn't filled the prescriptions I'd given him. Laurie said they'd picked up the meds for him, but he never took them. I was pleased to hear about their efforts, but it was a small comfort. We'd all been trying to help but, in the end, it was probably

Paris's mental illness that allowed his paranoia of hospitals and medicines to thrive.

I should have pushed harder. Today, I would have prioritized treating his mental illness by starting a long-acting injectable antipsychotic (which wasn't available then). Thankfully, these medications have become life savers. Patients can take a shot twice a year to avoid their delusions and paranoia. Unfortunately, California's definition of grave disability does not include the inability to take care of one's severe medical needs. Some other states include this in the definition.

Today, I'm more knowledgeable about the laws and would have insisted that Paris was a danger to self. I don't think he wanted to die, but he had a deep-seated fear of medications and hospitals. Today, I would ask, "Why don't you want to take medications or stay in the hospital?" And if his answer exhibited paranoia or delusions, he could have been deemed incapable of making medical decisions for himself. That process should have happened when he was first hospitalized. But when no one is advocating for a patient like Paris, releasing the patient is much easier than trying to place him on a hold. And even if he had been placed on a hold, a psychiatric hospital wouldn't have accepted someone with medical needs. You see, there aren't enough psychiatric hospital beds for those experiencing acute crises, and there aren't enough "step down" facilities for sub-acute issues. Furthermore, healthy residential living facilities for people with severe mental illness are severely lacking. At every level, there's a bottleneck. Consequently, if someone wants to leave the hospital, there isn't much incentive to work hard to keep them against their will, unless you're a good doctor!

Losing Paris was frustrating and disheartening. He had died in his sleep, in the apartment provided by the Full-Service Partnership Program.

When I told James, the director of the Needle Exchange, about Paris, he lowered his head. "That's a bummer," he said. "I had brought him a bunch of socks I accidentally turned pink in the wash."

I looked at him and smiled. "He would have really liked that."

14

TREAT, DON'T INCARCERATE

WHEN WORKING AT THE LOS ANGELES COUNTY WOMEN'S JAIL as a primary care physician, I went to visit Amelia (not her real name) in the highest level of mental illness housing. Inmates are separated into "general population," low-level, and high-level mental illness housing. The high-level mentally ill are most vulnerable for death while incarcerated. I had a careful look at each high-level inmate I saw. The prison mental health team was worried about Amelia because she was catatonic and hadn't been eating. She was on a list for admittance to the Forensic Inpatient Unit (FIP), which usually has a two-to-three-week wait because there are only forty-two beds available for twenty thousand inmates.

Until Amelia was admitted into FIP, she couldn't be treated against her will. She was in a single cell when I stopped by. She was muscular, around thirty years old, with black, short hair. She stood like a robot, not moving, wearing only a sports bra and nothing else.

I stood outside the cell and spoke to her through an opening in the door. "Hi Amelia," I said slowly. "My name is Dr. Partovi. How are you? I've come to check on you."

No response. She continued staring into space without acknowledging my presence.

"Amelia, is there anything I can help you with?"

No response. She didn't move at all. Custody had been concerned that she'd been that way for days.

I went back to speak to the staff. I asked them to remove her from the cell and bring her to the clinic. I knew it was a big ask. For good reason, custody is resistant to forcibly extracting inmates from their cells. But they saw I was serious and worried, and they brought her out.

In the clinic, we were able to take vitals and examine her. Her blood pressure was dangerously low, and her heart rate was high. This indicated severe dehydration. She was transferred to the Los Angeles County/USC Medical Center, where there is a ward for inmates. At the hospital, they discovered she was in kidney failure from being so dehydrated. They "tuned her up" by giving IV fluids but also treated her catatonia, which is a type of schizophrenia. Within a few days, she was walking, talking, eating, and drinking on her own.

Now, I don't know why Amelia was arrested. The mental health team is usually aware and in the cases I had encountered, arrests were always for something stupid—minor, nonviolent. Yes, I believe it's stupid to arrest a severely mentally ill person when they are suffering severe symptoms. Often, they were arrested for trespassing—being somewhere they weren't supposed to be. And when others tried to force them to leave, they became irritable and caused trouble. Police will call this "resisting" or "being threatening" when really, they are responding to a perceived threat.

When someone with severe mental illness (e.g., schizophrenia, bipolar disorder) is arrested, if the police suspect physical injury or some other medical concern, they take the person to the nearest emergency room to get "cleared" medically. If someone is having a heart attack, for example, they will stay in the hospital for treatment until they are no longer at risk. Then, they can be cleared to face the charges for whatever they've done.

Recently, a psychiatrist colleague of mine was working at an emergency room, where he consulted on an arrested individual. His assessment was that the individual was having an acute psychotic episode and needed to be emergently hospitalized. But the police officer retorted, "Crime trumps crazy!"—meaning, psychiatric emergencies can be addressed in jail. Someone having a heart attack can stay in the hospital for treatment, but someone having a psychiatric episode doesn't get this consideration. This is discrimination.

In prison, inmates suffering life-threatening psychosis—like Amelia— cannot get treatment until they're admitted to the forty-two-bed, FIP hospital. Of the twenty thousand inmates in L.A. County's jail system, 20 percent are mentally ill. So, four thousand inmates have access to forty-two beds in a psychiatric hospital.

Once, I was taking care of an inmate who had exhibited suicidal tendencies. I believed she needed to be hospitalized, just like someone with a dire, medical need for hospitalization. After many phone calls, the answer remained "no." We placed this inmate in a high-level housing and put her on suicide watch. This means a single cell, with no clothes or underwear (which could be used for hanging). The inmate gets a "suicide gown," a blanket of sorts, connected with Velcro together like a dress but lacking arms. Custody checks on these inmates every fifteen minutes. This is NOT adequate treatment for someone who is so depressed they are considering suicide. In fact, I believe it's barbaric.

Thankfully, in March of 2020, the Los Angeles County Board of Supervisors adopted strategies to create alternatives to incarceration for the mentally ill and have instructed teams to produce answers. In the meantime, we should be treating the severely mentally ill BEFORE they become incarcerated! This often requires treatment against the patient's will, which some believe is unjust. Why is it acceptable to jail them in the full throes of their illness, causing such extreme suffering? They should be considered gravely disabled, but our system isn't equipped to handle so many gravely disabled. Thus, psychiatrists are forced to raise the bar for grave disability.

Furthermore, if a psychiatrist deems that a patient needs a conservator (someone to be a guardian and make decisions for them), the hospital must care for the patient until a locked facility is available. This can take up to nine months. The cost of care in a long-term care facility is one-third the cost of hospitalization at a medical hospital. California needs more long-term facility beds and a funding stream to pay for them. Medicaid does not pay for long-term psychiatric care. We need to stop discriminating against the mentally ill and most importantly, provide psychiatric care instead of jail time. Treat don't incarcerate.

15

IT'S NOT OKAY WITH MY SOUL

I met Barbara in 2014, when I started going out with my medical team on the streets of LA's Skid Row. She stood out because she was an older woman living by herself in the thick of the "heroin district." She had long dreads and dirty clothes but always greeted us with a shy smile, like she was embarrassed about her overlapping front teeth. She seemed frail and spoke with tenderness. She broke my heart. She broke all our hearts.

Barbara was willing to talk to us but unwilling to come to the clinic a few blocks away "Who will watch my stuff?" she would ask. Barbara always stayed close to the same corner, Sixth and Stanford, where she'd sit surrounded by loads of her stuff. She never had much to say, but when asked how she was doing, she would always say "fine." Sometimes, she'd ask for skin cream and pain pills for her arthritis. I didn't suspect a serious medical condition, but she obviously wasn't able to take proper care of herself.

The legal definition for grave disability in California is someone with a mental disorder who is unable to provide food, clothing, or shelter for themself. Barbara was unable to maintain a safe shelter environment. Barbara's makeshift dwelling had a cardboard floor and a tarp for a roof; eventually, she acquired a tent like the rest of the Skid Row inhabitants. But she was still exposed to the winter cold and summer heat, along with predators, vermin, and illness. One of my teammates found out she used to live in the hotel across the street from her current spot, but she'd been kicked out years before for hoarding and failing to maintain a livable apartment.

She hadn't gone far. As the outreach team began to focus more and more on housing for PEH, Barbara received the grandest prize, an apartment at the beautiful Star Apartments a few blocks away. But she refused to go and couldn't tell us why.

I'm a family physician who specializes in street medicine, which is what it sounds like—I take care of patients in the streets. A group of people such as social workers, mental health clinicians, medical clinicians, nurses, and outreach workers look for the most vulnerable "rough sleepers" (those who refuse to enter shelters) and attempt to woo them into accepting help for whatever they need. The ultimate goal is getting them into housing, with the support they need to stay healthy and happy. You might ask yourself why we should care if Barbara—and thousands like her—are living on the streets if that's their wish.

I think about my mom. I wouldn't say she was severely mentally ill; after all, she was a high school English teacher in the Los Angeles Unified School District for decades. We had a strained relationship, both when I was growing up and later, when I became an adult. She was cantankerous, selfish, and often mean. Moreover, she would lie and all her life, was a hoarder. As a result, I didn't speak to her for eleven years. It felt like it was too hard to be her daughter. But in 2005, I took a course that helped me to take a fresh look at how I'd interpreted my past. I realized that I didn't have to allow my mom's behavior to affect me or maintain power over me. I reached out to her, saying I was ready to have her back in my life. "Thank God!" she said. "You've made me suffer for so long!"

I knew she would never change, but I was the one who had changed. I had to accept her for all she was and all she wasn't. We reunited, but I still didn't spend much time with her—mostly holidays and birthdays. We didn't talk on the phone regularly, but when we did speak, I noticed that she'd often repeat herself. She'd tell the same stories over and over.

One day, I received a call that she had fallen and broken her arm. She required surgery. While she was in the hospital, it became evident to the hospital staff that she had severe dementia. I went to her condo and found a complete mess. There were unpaid bills and taxes, and trash and rotting food everywhere. That was in 2009. I took over her care, which included hiring live-in caretakers. At first, she resisted. "I don't need anyone living here!" she'd say. I told her she needed them because of her arm. By the time she was healed, she'd become accustomed to their presence and seemed to appreciate the company. Once on a trip to the bank, the teller asked about the woman accompanying us, and my mom quickly answered, "My caretaker!" She had finally accepted them.

Over the years, my mother slowly deteriorated. Eventually, she didn't know her address, her age, or at times, my name. It's easy to imagine that if I had not stepped in, she could have lost her condominium due to unpaid taxes. This, along with her mental state, could have led her to life on the streets. Though demented, my mom remained feisty and didn't like being told what to do, or even touched. She would have deflected attempts at help from anyone outside the family—just like many of the PEH I encounter.

Despite my issues with my mom, I would have NEVER allowed her to sleep in a tent exposed to the horrors of homelessness. I don't care how much she would have protested. She could have cussed me out, hit me, or worse; I would NEVER have allowed her to be homeless. It wouldn't have been okay with my soul. Why do I care about Barbara? Do I see Barbara as my mom? No, but she could be someone else's mom, or daughter, or sister. It just isn't okay with my soul.

Although I suspected that Barbara had some sort of mental illness, she didn't seem delusional or talk to people who weren't there. Most likely, she had dementia. I asked one of our outreach nurses to do a dementia test on her and she scored exceptionally low. But because Barbara had refused housing, the outreach workers had little hope of getting her help. By the time I heard this, I had changed positions and hadn't been doing outreach work, so Barbara was no longer on my radar.

In 2018, the Los Angeles County supervisor, Kathryn Barger, expressed interest publicly in caring for the gravely disabled PEH, so I offered to give her a tour of Skid Row. I found Supervisor Barger to be concerned and caring, someone who sincerely wanted to see change in how severely mentally ill PEH were treated. When we met, she was perfectly made up and wore a white button-down blouse, but she had put on walking shoes. She listened intently to everything I told her. After trudging through the tent-filled sidewalks and speaking to many PEH, I introduced her to Barbara. Younger than she looked, Barbara had a direct and sweet demeanor. She was someone whose vulnerability came through, even though she didn't really seem to mind living on Skid Row. Supervisor Barger was visibly affected by meeting her.

The next day, Supervisor Barger expressed her concerns at the weekly meeting of supervisors and her desire to expand California's definition of grave disability to include the inability to care for one's medical conditions. And so began California's legislative process to expand this definition and introduce the idea that we need to take care of these people, even against their will. Unfortunately, this bill never made it beyond our state congress, so we continue to have the LPS Act that doesn't protect the Barbaras of the world.

Soon afterward, an outreach nurse I knew texted to tell me that Barbara had been admitted to a recuperative care facility. These are specifically for vulnerable PEH, used as transitional housing until the arrangement of something more permanent. The outreach team saw a window of opportunity; the guy that "helped" Barbara out on the streets had cancer, and when he entered a recuperative care facility, Barbara had agreed to go with him. This is a common scenario, a helpless woman receiving SSI benefits suddenly has a "boyfriend" or "husband" who claims to take care of her but really helps himself to her monthly check. Often, the women become dependent and don't want to accept housing without them.

At the time, I had been working with DMH (LA County's Department of Mental Health), helping to create a street psychiatry program along with a psychiatrist, Dr. Jones, to assist the gravely disabled on the streets. I called Dr. Jones and told him about Barbara. A few days later, we met her at the facility. It was even more obvious that her inability to care for herself was due to her dementia, as she wandered the facility claiming other people's clothes as her own. She exhausted the workers and needed constant redirecting. Dr. Jones recommended a dementia ward, which is a locked facility. A week later, Barbara was accepted to a locked board and care. A nurse colleague sent me a video of her playing with other housemates, passing a big beach ball back and forth and laughing.

The medical community has long accepted that people with dementia need an exceedingly high level of care and can't be allowed to leave their current facility, for fear of harm to self. However, people with severe mental illness suffer discrimination in this regard. Our society believes that those suffering from psychiatric illnesses can make decisions about their own care but in fact, those with untreated psychosis cannot. They lack the ability to make rational decisions and are subject to self-harm as a result. By law, every psychotic person living on the streets qualifies as gravely disabled, which calls for immediate action. They should be hospitalized, stabilized, and supported until they can live a life of peace, purpose, comfort, safety, and joy. Psychiatric illnesses should be viewed in the same urgent light as medical illnesses that cause an inability to care for oneself. Whether someone is in danger because of dementia, paranoia, or a medical condition, the danger of harm and suffering is high.

It can be difficult to discern exactly *why* someone is unable to practice self-care. One patient I saw regularly at the Center for Harm Reduction was hospitalized frequently for severe paranoia that caused her to threaten others. She had been beaten or raped several times, sometimes after putting herself in harm's way. Usually this occurred when she was using methamphetamines.

Another patient I saw in the women's jail started having delusions and paranoia in her fifties (usually psychiatric conditions don't start that late in life). She showed improvement on psychiatric medications, but after much investigation and laboratory testing, we discovered she had lupus, which was causing her psychotic symptoms. It shouldn't really matter. Whether due to dementia, lupus, drug use, or schizophrenia—these are examples of people who couldn't take care of themselves. We need to stop discriminating against those with severe mental illness and treat it like the brain disease it is. It's up to us, their community, to take care of them as if they're family.

16

NEW KID; GOOD DOCTOR

ONE DAY, I SAW THIS NEW KID AT MY CLINIC AT THE NEEDLE
Exchange. His dark blonde hair was going in all different directions,
the bangs covering his eyes. His head was down, arms crossed, giving
off that teenage, *I-hate-everyone* aura. As I stepped over to where he
perched on the edge of a chair, I could almost imagine his thoughts: "I
know you think I'm a shit. I hate being here, but I have no choice. I'm
sick." I asked him questions, and he responded in monosyllables, with
attitude, as if he'd been called into the principal's office.

In residency, I learned that how *you* feel in the presence of a
patient is most likely how *they* feel. In this case, the kid was probably
the one who thought he was a shit. Up to that point in his life, plenty
of others had made him believe it.

People are, in many ways, a product of their interactions with
other people. Especially parents. When my mother was upset with
something I'd done, she would say things like "If I had said that to my
father, I would have been thrown down the stairs," or, "You're lucky
you didn't grow up in my house. You would've been beaten to a pulp."

Harriett Shrybman was born March 13, 1936, in Buffalo, New York. Her father, Joseph Shrybman, and mother, Sarah Miller, were both raised in Canada. Joseph immigrated to Canada from Ukraine (then part of Russia) at two years of age, during the pogroms. He came with his father, Samuel, and eventually the entire family arrived in the U.S. in 1915. Joseph had a twin brother, Jack, whom my mom adored. My grandma died when I was six, and my grandpa when I was twelve. I remember visiting them in Buffalo around the age of three. I was the center of attention, adorable in my fuchsia skirt and white patterned tights. My mom's younger brothers were there, Alfred and Mike. My uncle Mike was later diagnosed with schizophrenia and lived in a "home." One of my mom's cousins, Uncle Jack's son, also was schizophrenic and disappeared for several years. I knew little about my own uncles and wished I could have been part of their lives. But my mom hated Buffalo, and we only visited twice. When I was cleaning up her condominium in 2019 after I moved her to a group home, I found many photos of her brothers. She must have loved them, but she never talked about her siblings much. She remained guarded about her past.

When I asked the new kid why he had come to the clinic, he showed me an abscess on his abdomen. It was big, about the size of an orange, very warm and very red. "Is it painful?" I asked, and he nodded without looking at me. I begin to ask my usual questions: *Last Hepatitis C test? Last HIV test? Last TB test? Any past medical history?*

He answered each question in staccato, never raising his eyes to meet mine. It's possible he'd had negative experiences with doctors in the past, or with adults in general. I began to feel like an interrogator, although I tried to speak in my normal, upbeat tone. I could sense he was waiting for me to chastise him, to say, "How dare you treat your body this way!" Or, to tell him he must stop using drugs. "Look, see what drugs do to you?! You're an idiot if you continue after this!" I imagined these thoughts swirling around in his head because he'd heard it all before. On some level, he believed these statements to be true.

My mom could be quite condescending towards me. I think she was jealous of my dad's affection for me or just jealous in general. Though I knew my dad loved me, he never said it until I was nineteen years old. As I grew up, I believed I was a brat—difficult and basically, unlovable. Now I see that my mom felt that way about herself and didn't know how to nurture me. And yet, she was a high school teacher in South Central LA. Once while seeing patients at MLK Urgent Care, a patient said, "Dr. Partovi? Any relation to Harriett Partovi?" When I told him that she was my mom, the now-thirty-something-year-old said, "She was my favorite teacher!" So, she'd figured out how to make an impact on other kids, I guess.

As I prepared to open the new kid's abscess, I asked, "Do you usually skin pop?" I was referring to the method of using drugs by injecting under the skin.

"Uh, no. I usually mainline." This meant he injected directly into his veins. "But I was desperate," he added.

As I painted his purplish lesion with a brown-orange cleaning agent, I said, "Next time, when you can't find a vein, muscle it." This means injecting into muscle instead of skin. "But you'll need a longer needle," I said. "I'll get you some."

He raised his head and looked at me directly for the first time. He had clear brown eyes, and long eyelashes wasted on a boy. His chart said he was twenty years old.

At that moment, I saw what I see in the eyes of every drug user I treat. The slow dawning of the realization that someone is really seeing them. Their backs straighten a little and their eyes brighten when they realize that maybe, just maybe, they are someone worthy of respect, worthy of someone's concern and time. Just worthy.

There are shitty doctors who won't give adequate pain control to drug users in the hospital. "Just give them ibuprofen," they'll say, as if treating a patient's pain would be somehow condoning their addiction. I've seen doctors who take it upon themselves to punish patients for using drugs. A shitty doctor would think that treating a drug user for a self-inflicted wound was a waste of their time. Guess what? These patients know what the shitty doctor believes about them. Over time, it's what prevents patients like this new kid from seeking medical care at all. They begin to absorb the idea that they're unworthy, that they really are a piece of shit.

I related to new kid because we all grow up with confidence issues related to being worthy or "good enough." Family is supposed to encourage and teach us to be confident in ourselves. I would say that a good amount of PEH and/or drug users were missing that support in their lives in some way. In fact, most have experienced an insurmountable amount of trauma in their lives. As an adult, I know my parents and family loved me, but as a child, we didn't verbally express love, and I often felt unlovable. Even now, that feeling seeps into my thoughts unconsciously from time to time. I imagine that's how many of my patients feel. I use food to make me feel better; they use heroin or other substances. Food is slightly more acceptable in our society! I've done a lot of interpersonal work on myself and learned that being aware of these thoughts that sneak up is key. When we numb ourselves with our addictions, we can't recognize and intercept those thoughts and say, "This is not true," and "I choose to stand for love and joy, passion and compassion." This is the real truth I wish my patients could experience.

I gave the new kid local anesthesia, making sure the area was numb. "Are you okay?" I asked.

"Yeah."

"Do you feel this?"

"No."

My mom told me that she had run away with her teenage boyfriend, Henry Klein, as soon as she turned eighteen. From looking at the photographs I found in her condominium, it seemed they lived with his parents. Henry's father was a rabbi and his mother had was a Holocaust survivor who was missing her right forearm—supposedly, amputated by the Nazis. When I showed the photos to my Uncle Alfred (now Abraham after becoming an orthodox Jew and moving to Israel), he had fond memories of his sister's in-laws. It makes me happy to think that my mom's in-laws acted as substitute parents. They all moved to Seattle, and my mother had Gerry in 1955 and Michelle in 1962. The in-laws are still present in my mom's photographs up until Michelle is about two or three. My mother met my father at a folk dancing event in Los Angeles, and they were married in Las Vegas on October 1, 1966. My half-siblings stayed with their father. I have no idea what happened to end my mother's first marriage, or why and how she ended up in Los Angeles. I was my parents' only child.

When I was nineteen, my father told me that he and my mother were getting divorced. And for the first time, he told me the story of their courtship and early marriage. "When she was pregnant with you," he said, "I was so much in love with her." He told me that his mother saw bruises on my body once when I was a baby, and he told my mom he would kill her if he ever saw that again. Over time, his love for her turned to hate. "In those days," he said, "the mother would get the children after a divorce. I couldn't risk that." I often wish he would have left her, because the ensuing years were filled with so much anger, jealousy, competition, and pain.

"I'm going to make an incision now," I told the new kid. The skin around the abscess, just below his ribcage, was pale and smooth and hadn't been exposed much to the sun. As I cut, I asked again, "Are you okay?"

"Yeah," he responded, but more softly now.

I continued to walk him through what I was doing, constantly asking for feedback as I performed the procedure. He no longer muttered his answers or hid behind his bangs. He became a "normal" person.

I have always believed that if you treat someone as if he's an animal, he will show up as an animal. If you treat him like a kind, respectful human being, he will show up as a kind, respectful human being. And guess what? The patient knows what the good doctor believes about him, too. One day, with enough encouragement, he can learn to believe good things about himself.

People naturally gravitate to positive and encouraging people, I believe. Everyone wants to feel acceptance and love. During my childhood, I gravitated to the immediate area of my neighborhood when things at home felt lacking. I met the Rochelles when I was seven. Tiffany Rochelle became my best friend, and our parents didn't care for each other. In fact, my mother was very jealous of Tiffany's mom. Jan Rochelle was a tall, beautiful redhead who became a mother figure for all the kids on Dorothy Street, where we lived. She was a great cook and allowed candy, cookies, and chips! The Rochelle house became the block's new hangout and my sanctuary.

At the end of the block were the Gunthers. The father, Gary, drank a lot of beer and would pay us to crush the aluminum cans so he could recycle them. Aaron and Mark were two boys who lived in the apartment building across the street. I had my first French kiss with Aaron at thirteen and would chase that sexual feeling for the rest of my life! In a yellow house, also across the street, lived Sue (Big Sue, we called her, and I was Little Sue or Susie). She lived with her toddler son, John, and her mother. Little John's dad was Big John, who didn't live with them but was the dad of Dorothy Street, nonetheless. At neighborhood gatherings, he'd cook his famous grilled chicken. When a blonde girl moved in, we found out that Big John had another daughter, Tiffany, and her mother had died in a car accident. Sue took "Little Tiff" in and became a stepmother to her.

The two Tiffanys—Big Tiff and Little Tiff—and I did everything together, hanging out and sharing clothes. Little Tiff looked like a shorter Christie Brinkley but seemed insecure, which baffled us. Boys followed her around and she seemed completely indifferent. She attended a private school so during the school year, I didn't see her much.

I spent most of my free time at the Rochelle house with Big Tiff. My mom was jealous of my relationship with Jan, who was just easy to be around. She never judged me or made me feel less. Hers was the house I started cleaning for ten dollars a week, an offer Jan made after she saw that I didn't have enough clothes. With my first payment, I bought a pair of brown corduroy, flared Sassoon pants, half off at Horizons, where all the rich kids bought their clothes in Brentwood.

A South African family moved in down the street. The father was a yogi to the stars and always wore white garments. The wife was funny and beautiful and had a closet full of amazing clothes. Big Tiff, Little Tiff and I started babysitting for them. This was when I truly decided to dress with flare—clothes, shoes, and jewelry. Just like Jackie!

When my mom found out I'd started babysitting, she had a fit. She had started traveling to the east coast during my summer vacations. My father and I got along better when she was gone. No weird rules, no yelling, no tantrums, no silent treatment, no jealousy, no drama. When I told my dad I was going to babysit, there was no discussion. He trusted me.

"Who said you can do that?" my mom asked.

I made my own decisions and my own money. I was in charge of my own life. "Me," I said.

"A twelve-year-old can't babysit!" she said.

"Yes, I can. I've been doing it for two months already."

She raised her voice. "Over my dead body! You will never go there again!"

I might have said something like "Fuck you," and she chased me out of the house with a broom. I don't remember where I went, probably to Big Tiff's. Back then, I often fantasized about running away. But I knew I couldn't take care of myself, not yet.

When I was growing up, I was affected by the words and actions of those around me—my family, my parents, and especially, my mother. I sometimes felt unworthy of love or respect and to this day, I become triggered when someone doesn't show me respect.

I've never lived on the streets and my only addictions are food-related, but I do understand the need to be treated with respect. If you heard that your mother was in an emergency room, you wouldn't want her to be disrespected or made to feel less than because of an illness. You'd want her to have compassion, pain relief, whatever she needed. You'd want her to be treated how family *should* treat each other, with love.

I finished cleaning up the abscess on the new kid, then gently wrapped it. Gingerly, he lowered his shirt back over his abdomen. As he left, he looked me in the eyes. "Thank you," he said, this time clearly.

"You're very welcome," I replied, and I made sure to look right back at him, eye-to-eye.

17

TINA MARIE

"BYE, BYE, MISS AMERICAN PIE."

Tina sang along with the radio as I worked on her leg. She had an abscess, one of many I had treated over the years. She was a heroin user and a regular at the Needle Exchange. One of our more difficult clients, she had severe mental health issues, could be scattered when trying to communicate, and often wouldn't keep the appointments we set up for her. We had tried sending her to a mental health clinic, the local medical clinic, the DMV to get an ID—you name it. She couldn't keep an appointment. We tried to set her up with disability benefits, but she never showed up for the appointments with the psychiatrist or the caseworker. She would, however, come to the Needle Exchange religiously to take advantage of whatever we had going on that day— groups, acupuncture, art classes. She'd accept and eat a sandwich, wait to see me, and then quickly be on her way. If we hadn't seen her in a while, it meant she was in jail.

"I drove my Chevy to the levy, but the levy was dry—"

When I first met her, Tina was very thin. She wore dirty clothes, and her greasy blond hair covered her face. At first, she didn't talk much. Her head protruded forward, like a turtle, making her gait seem off balance. "Kola," a beautiful blond retriever and shepherd mix, often accompanied her. She tied a red sweatshirt around his neck for a leash. For a year, he never left her side. He was a sweet boy, around four years old and would chew his paws often.

Over time, she became more comfortable with us. She talked more and often was quite animated. At times, she could even be playful and child-like. I offered to take Kola to the vet for vaccines.

On the day I was supposed to bring him back, Tina was nowhere to be found. One of the clients overheard us asking about her and said, "Oh, she's in the hospital. She broke her neck!" I called the county hospital and sure enough, she was in the ICU.

It turned out that she had held her head funny due to a vertebral abscess (infection in the spine) which had caused severe disruption of the bone. She had fallen, breaking her neck where that old infection was. The infection had been caused by bacteria from injecting heroin.

I kept the dog, renaming him Koda.

"—and good ole boys were drinking whisky and rye."

Tina was hospitalized and sent to nine months of rehabilitation for her spine injuries following surgery. When she showed up back at the Needle Exchange, she was back on the streets and in a wheelchair, using heroin again. She was back to her disheveled, scattered self. I continued to see her for various reasons over the next year.

During one visit, I noticed her belly was getting bigger. She was conversant, but mostly because I had Koda and she asked about him, but she was still exhibiting scattered thinking. We had a bond at that point and could talk about anything. She never did ask for Koda back and said he was better off with me. Insights like that raised my regard for her. I could tell she was embarrassed about being back on the streets.

"Tina, are you drinking?" I asked.

"Yeah, a pint a day."

I knew she had hepatitis C, which can often cause cirrhosis, a scarring of the liver. Drinking dramatically increases one's risk of cirrhosis and end-stage liver disease. *Crap*, I thought. Excessive alcohol does a lot of damage to the body, especially alongside hepatitis C, and the risk of overdose greatly increases if the patient takes other substances. Tina's combined heroin and alcohol use was extremely dangerous. Every time I saw her, her belly looked bigger. I referred her to various specialty clinics, but she never showed up.

"—singing, this will be the day that I die."

After living with me for two-and-a-half years, Koda was diagnosed with lymphoma. He was only six years old. During those last few months while he was on chemotherapy, I often brought him to the Needle Exchange, hoping Tina would be able to see him. I didn't tell her he was sick; he didn't look sick. I wanted her to fully enjoy him. She saw Koda several times, loving him up, petting and kissing him, almost like a loving mom.

After Koda passed, I didn't see Tina for a couple of months.

When I did see her, I took her into my office and began to weep. I had never cried in front of one of my patients before. I told her that Koda had passed away from cancer, that I had done everything I could, but the cancer was too strong. She started to cry, too. I kept saying, "I'm sorry." She patted my hand and told me that giving him to me was the best thing she had done. She saw that he was incredibly happy with me. At that point, I realized she was the one consoling me.

Because of our connection through Koda, Tina had become family. I appreciated her love and care for him. She had given him up so he could receive proper care—in that way, we were the same. She was a loving mom and had allowed me to be Koda's auntie. I'll be forever grateful for her gift.

Tina's belly continued to grow, and the rest of her body swelled with water retention. She became visibly short of breath. I told her she needed to go to the hospital. She had always been resistant, but this time, she went.

Her caseworker called to tell me Tina wasn't doing well. I went to the hospital, fearing the worst. But when I saw Tina, she wore a clean hospital gown, and her hair was wet from a shower. Her swelling seemed much improved.

I had another trick up my sleeve. LA County's Integrative Mental Health Program was specifically for mentally ill PEH with substance abuse problems and chronic medical conditions. I talked to Tina about her mental health issues.

"Tina, why do you think you use and drink? Are you depressed?"

With more clarity than ever, she looked at me. "Yeah, for a long time now."

I'm not a therapist and didn't want to delve into her past trauma, but I could feel it in her. She had some psychosis, too, based on her hygiene and scattered thinking. I urged my contacts to see her while she was in the hospital, because it was so difficult to pin her down on the streets. I had to make a case for her, try to convince them she was a viable candidate. I made calls and sent emails to the head of a mental health agency. Eventually, she was accepted into the program.

After her hospitalization, Tina stayed for about a month in recuperative care (post-hospital care for PEH). Eventually, she left and showed up at the Needle Exchange. I called her caseworker, who, within ten minutes, arrived and whisked Tina off to emergency housing! Later, Tina came back with her caseworker and a psychiatric nurse practitioner who reviewed all her medications, including psychiatric medications. We all wanted to be on the same page. It was nice to finally be able to make plans for Tina's care and know they would be carried out. Tina followed along in the discussion, somewhat, but seemed happy to let us figure out her needs. This team was helping with medications and making sure she was showing up for appointments.

Before they left, Tina lifted her arm to show me a treasured possession: her laminated ID fashioned into a large bracelet. Without it, she couldn't get into her housing.

"Check it out, Dr. P!" She smiled broadly. "I'm never losing this!"

Finally, all her needs were being met. She was getting ready to move into permanent housing.

"I deserve this," she said, her smile fading. "I've led a hard life."

I smiled back, nodding in agreement.

"So, bye, bye Miss American Pie, drove my Chevy to the levy, but the levy was dry. And good ole boys were drinking whisky and rye singing this'll be the day that I die. This'll be the day that I die."

On my birthday in 2012, I was having a particularly difficult day. I had found out that one of our Needle Exchange patients had died, and one of my mentally ill homeless patients in the hospital was refusing all care. As I was waiting for the microwave to *ding* my lunch ready, one of our caseworkers came in. She said that Tina had just come in to tell me she was in her own apartment. She wanted to thank me. I nodded and thanked the caseworker. *Finally. She deserves this.* This could be an important first step to getting Tina the treatment she needed and closer to a better life.

Five months later, the caseworker called. "Did you hear about Tina?"

Fearing the worst, I sat down. "What happened?"

"She passed away last week."

She died in her apartment. I wept.

"This'll be the day that I die."

Tina was ill on so many levels and yet, she made us laugh and laughed with us. I knew she would die soon, as she had end stage liver disease. She needed a new liver, but with her history, wasn't a candidate for transplant. Finally, she received the support she needed and was able to live out her last months comfortably. For Tina and all PEH, being able to spend their last months or years at home is truly a gift. They deserve it. But for most of her life, Tina felt she didn't deserve to be taken care of. Whatever her past traumas were, they taught her she was worthless, less than, a piece of shit. And she believed it. She believed it until we took care of her. With time, she began to believe she was worthy of love, care, and happiness. I have a picture of Tina outside the Needle Exchange. She'd visit often after she started living in her own place. She had gained weight and cut her hair. She wore a tie-dyed purple T-shirt and looked right into the camera with a big smile on her face.

We often can't prevent PEH from dying after decades of physical harm to their bodies. But we can care for them the best we know how. We can allow their sparkle to shine through and live the time they have left with respect, kindness, and dignity.

18

SOMETIMES ROCK BOTTOM IS DEATH

IT WAS THE END OF THE DAY AT OUR PRIMARY CARE CLINIC IN Skid Row, and I was talking about my patient, George, a heroin user who lived in a tent. I met him while out practicing street medicine. "Sometimes," I said, "rock bottom is death."

George was in his sixties but looked older. Often, we'd find him "on the nod" in his wheelchair, so loaded he could barely stay awake, or sleeping in his tent. The year before, he'd been hit by a car and had suffered a broken hip. He'd never had rehab for it—thus, the wheelchair. He also had asthma. From the moment we met, I saw George as someone especially in danger: an older, homeless, chronically ill heroin user. He wouldn't look me in the eyes and seemed perpetually sleepy. Studies show that those who are experiencing homelessness with severe medical issues are most likely to die. PEH who are heroin users are nine times more likely to die than those who have housing.

Once, George asked me to refill the inhalers for his asthma. I called in the prescription to the local pharmacy, but he never picked them up. Several times, I tried to get him to come to the clinic three blocks away. He never did. Eventually, I started ordering his medications and picking them up myself. After work, I'd drive the few blocks to his tent and toss them to him from my car. There were other stopped cars on this route—except they were either dealers, or people picking up illicit drugs. George did start visiting the clinic after I had trimmed the corns from his buddy's feet. The two men would come together. During our ensuing visits, George told me he hated using heroin and wanted to start methadone, a replacement medication that helps detox from opiates. But he didn't have ID, which is required at the methadone clinic. And he couldn't get an ID, because it was too difficult for him to get to the DMV.

As his health continued to deteriorate, we got him placed into temporary housing. Twice, he was kicked out for using heroin and returned to his tent, where he could use freely. Sometimes he was so loaded he couldn't get back to the temporary housing. Sometimes, he said he was too sick. I treated George twice for walking pneumonia and I asked one of the clinic outreach nurses to start checking on him regularly. One day, she called to notify me that George's friend had told her they'd had to call 911 because he wouldn't wake up.

While George was still in the ER at LAC/USC, I called to check on him. It was bad. His liver had failed, his kidneys had failed, and he was septic (when bacteria get into your blood stream, causing blood pressure to drop dangerously low). He had been intubated. The doctors thought he may have overdosed. Over the following days, I continued to follow up on him. When one of my homeless patients is admitted to a hospital, I often see it as an opportunity to detox them, to get them into a nursing home or temporary housing and away from bad influences on the street. In George's case, it may have been too late.

That same day, Dennis came in. It was his second time at the clinic. We had first met him, months before, during our outreach at

Gladys Park in Skid Row. He wore a black T-shirt that made the large, gold, Star of David medallion around his neck stand out. The medallion became how I could identify and find him. After my initial greeting and questions, he told us he was HIV-positive and had liver cancer. He was being seen for his HIV at the AIDS Health Foundation, he said, but didn't know what to do to follow up on the liver cancer. He seemed lucid when describing his condition and what treatment he had received. Overall, he was much easier to engage with than George.

He signed a consent form allowing me to look up his medical records in the county system. At that time, I was working at the Star Clinic, a county facility right in Skid Row. And Dennis was right. He'd been diagnosed with liver cancer the year before, while in jail. He'd even had one round of chemotherapy before he was released. He told me he had refused surgery because he didn't have family around to help him through it. Since his release the summer before, he hadn't received any treatment.

We tried to get him into interim housing with nursing care, but he was hesitant because he, too, was a heroin user. It would be hard to be too far away from his epicenter of heroin availability, even though we assured him it was just one bus ride away. Still, he wouldn't go.

After that, I didn't see Dennis at the clinic for a while. He finally showed up a few months later, after a brief hospitalization for abdominal pain. Imaging showed that the tumor in his liver had become numerous tumors. My heart sank, knowing what that meant. He agreed to interim housing, and I procured an urgent oncology appointment within weeks.

Following his oncology appointment, I saw that they had ordered and scheduled more imaging. I asked Dennis to come back for a follow-up appointment with oncology in a month. I worried it would be too long and when he came back, he was in a lot of pain. He'd been hospitalized again, this time at a different hospital. He showed me the paperwork. I told him I would give him pain medication, but he couldn't use heroin with it.

"Don't you overdose on me!" I said, joking but also knowing it was a possibility. He chuckled and said he wouldn't. I asked him to come back a week later so I could check on him. Five days later, he was found in his room, unconscious and surrounded by needles. I didn't find out until a few days later, but the medical report looked bad. He was septic, with infections that often affect people with AIDs. The report said he'd stopped his HIV medications because they "hurt his stomach."

The hospital team was keeping him alive, but I didn't see any way out. Also, his liver cancer was so advanced, I wasn't sure it was worth it to be aggressive to keep him alive, if it would add to his quality of life. The staff had been trying to contact his family. I called a nurse from his HIV clinic and asked for Dennis's emergency contacts. She gave me his daughter's number and I called her. I left *that* message, the one every doctor hates. I had to tell her that her father was dying. I gave her the number to the hospital. She lived out of state but contacted them. Over the next few days, I spoke with the attending physician as we discussed Dennis's care. She claimed that his daughter was in the loop.

When Dennis left my office that last time, I turned to my resident and said, "Next time, I will discuss end-of-life issues." Part of me knew I should have broached the subject then. Although I've been a doctor for over twenty years and instruct students and residents about end-of-life conversations, it's still incredibly difficult for me to broach the subject. I can't help thinking about previous patients of mine who have died, and I also relive my dad's final months. When it comes time to have *that* talk with patients, I know it's the right thing to do, and yet, sometimes I procrastinate.

A few days later, the attending physician called to let me know that Dennis's daughter had decided to withdraw the medications keeping him alive. She couldn't travel to his bedside. He died soon afterwards, without any family around. He was fifty-four.

I received a call about another one of my patients. Casey was in the hospital again, and his case manager wanted me to try to convince him to enter a nursing home. An affable man in his sixties, Casey used to be homeless but was currently housed with wrap-around services; this type of housing includes staff who check on the residents regularly. I had been seeing him at the clinic for about a year. He had emphysema and heart failure and was on a regimen of heart medications and inhalers. From what I could tell, he was taking his medications regularly, but he still smoked cigarettes and had no desire to quit. He also drank alcohol, "a few drinks a week if I have money." A few months before, he'd been hospitalized for a skin infection, which I continued to treat.

A few weeks after he left the hospital, Casey came to the clinic with his case manager. He still had an infection, but he was tremulous and didn't sound completely lucid. His leg was still swollen and red. When I asked if he was drinking, he said yes, until he'd run out of money a few days before. His heartbeat was fast. I was concerned that he was in alcohol withdrawal, which can be potentially life-threatening. I called 911, and he was hospitalized.

After he'd been discharged again, Casey returned to the clinic with his caseworker, complaining of the same symptoms. The caseworker told me that Casey's apartment had recently caught on fire, and when the firefighters arrived, Casey was passed out. They found him confused and disheveled. I called 911 again and pressed the team to put him into a nursing home.

But when he was better, he refused to enter a nursing home and wouldn't stop drinking. He missed a follow-up appointment with me and ended up in the hospital again. His heart was so weak that during his alcohol binges, it would develop an abnormal rhythm. I emailed his case manager, telling her that if he didn't stop drinking, he was going to die.

Usually, I'm not such a hard ass with patients who are substance users. But if Casey didn't stop, his death was imminent. He was discharged again before I could see him. I went instead to his tiny apartment downtown, along with his caseworker and one of my nurses. It was filthy, filled with cigarette butts, beer cans, and at least a hundred medicine bottles. Casey seemed embarrassed about the disarray, but we told him we would help. The nurse and I organized the medications for him. Then I arrived at a brilliant idea!

"Casey," I said, "if I gave you a prescription for Lorazepam to take three times a day, would you want to decrease your drinking?" Lorazepam is a medicine that can help someone detox from alcohol and prevents potential death.

He brightened up, nodding. "Yeah! That's what they give me in the hospital, and I do fine on it!"

I never wrote a prescription so fast! I texted his case manager a week later to see how Casey was, and she said he was doing great.

At his appointment at the clinic, he had a fresh haircut, his clothes were clean, and he seemed more lucid and alert.

I didn't want to ask, but I did. "Are you still drinking?"

"Yes," he said, "but only about five beers a day. I've given up vodka."

Halleluiah! I'll take five beers a day over several pints of vodka! This is the definition of "harm reduction." It wasn't a perfect solution for his medical care, but it would keep him out of the hospital and living happily.

What happened to George? That first day, I thought for sure he was near death. He was hospitalized for five weeks. I visited him a couple of times while he was there. He told me he wanted to try methadone, and said he wanted to live—sober. Miraculously, he made a full recovery and entered a county recuperative care center. One day, I was talking to one of his buddies at his old site on Sixth Street when a man jogged toward us. "Here's George," the friend said.

I couldn't believe what I was seeing. This was a younger-looking, newly shaved man *jogging* across the street! It was George! He was a different man! He was off heroin and doing great. He had housing. It had taken persistence, patience, and a chance. That's what street medicine is about, seeing the potential spark for a young, handsome man in a nodding, disheveled heroin user.

George, Dennis, and Casey were all severe substance users with serious medical conditions. Each was fragile, knocking on death's door. George didn't make it and eventually, died alone. His rock bottom was death, and that is my biggest heartache. But with creativity, persistence, and a "whatever-it-takes" resolve, Casey and George survived. George almost didn't survive his rock bottom. It took a lot of energy, will, and resources, but he made it to the other side of his addiction. Casey was not able to stop drinking hard liquor on his own; in his case, being housed wasn't enough. But with the help of detox medications and a village of support, he was able to survive. We can help deliver many of our fragile brothers and sisters to the other side, where they can live their best lives. That is my biggest source of joy.

19

TRAGEDIES AND TRIUMPHS

"DIXIE'S VERY UPSET RIGHT NOW," THE PSYCHIATRIST announced. "I told her she doesn't have the capacity to make her own decisions and can't leave the hospital."

It was Thursday, two days after my forty-fifth birthday. I was driving to the Needle Exchange from my home in Venice. We were talking about Dixie, a patient I had hospitalized at Cedars Sinai on Monday. I'd called to ask if Dixie had decided to allow a colonoscopy.

Dixie was a sixty-something, homeless woman I had met doing street outreach at a church in Hollywood. She came to see me complaining of leg pain. Her hair was stringy under a straw hat, and she had tied a large, shimmery red bow around her neck "to hide my neck folds," she said.

I went to the church weekly and over several meetings, I had the opportunity to get to know her. Dixie was intelligent and spoke colorfully, with a spark in her eye. Often, she'd talk about her work with the CIA, how the church was tapped, and the government was out to get her, and about the fact that all medicine caused cancer. She also had much to say about God and Jesus. She was a homeless, mentally ill, elderly woman in Los Angeles—one of many I had met. The last time I had seen her, she'd mentioned that she thought she had hemorrhoids, and I'd told her to come to my community clinic in Hollywood for an examination.

The following Tuesday, she came to the Los Angeles Free Clinic (now called the Saban Community Clinic) near the Beverly Center. We ran through a general checklist of health questions. She told me she had heart disease and nutritional problems and always felt fatigued. I checked her blood count. It was extremely low—in fact, with a count like hers, any clinician would hospitalize her for a transfusion and a work-up. She wanted me to check her "hemorrhoid." I looked at the resident working with me, thinking we didn't have much time, but we examined her anyway. She didn't have a hemorrhoid. In fact, she didn't seem to have an anus. Her entire bottom had become a huge, angry, oozy ulcer—most likely, cancer, which would also explain her low blood count. Later, I told the resident it was a good lesson about listening to the patient.

Dixie refused to go to the hospital, but she agreed to iron supplementation to treat her anemia and a follow-up appointment the next week. When she came back, her blood count was even lower. An elderly woman with an extremely low blood count and whatever was on her backside—I worried about cancer. I discussed the importance of trying to figure out what was wrong at the hospital.

"I'll think about it," she said. "I have to figure out what to do with my belongings."

A few days later, I saw her at the church. Again, I asked her about going to the hospital.

"Monday," she told me. "I'll be ready Monday."

I texted my hospitalist contact (a physician dedicated to treating hospitalized patients) and arranged for our caseworker to get her to the hospital on Monday. Dixie showed up at the church and was taken to the hospital and admitted. I visited her the next day and met the medical team and psychiatrists. Dixie said she wanted time to think about the colonoscopy. We talked about the possibility of cancer and asked her what she would do if that were the case.

In her calm way, she said, "I'd have to handle it." But she said she'd agree to cancer treatment, if needed.

But now Dixie was upset and wanting to leave the hospital. She had decided she didn't want the colonoscopy and could make her own decisions about her health. I hung up with the psychiatrist and twenty minutes later, as I walked through the door of our clinic in Skid Row, I was on the phone with Dixie, trying to calm her down. "We're all worried about you," I told her. "We don't want you to leave the hospital without proper follow-up."

She was quite angry. After someone told her she shouldn't make her own decisions, she seemed unable to listen to anything else.

I called the psychiatric resident back and told him that although Dixie had been deemed incapacitated by psychiatry, I couldn't force her to stay in the hospital against her will. I had decided to trust that if I gave her room to think about the colonoscopy or even just a biopsy, she'd come to the decision on her own. I asked him to call me back with any updates.

My first patient at the Needle Exchange that day was Lucia, a young woman who had come in two days before to have her abscess opened by my colleague. That day, she had come for a dressing change.

Teddy, a pre-med volunteer, came in to update me while I worked on Lucia. "By the way, Dr. Partovi, I followed up with Betty and Ernesto on Tuesday."

My colleague, Dr. Tringale, and I ran a heroin detox program at the Needle Exchange. Then, we were the only program in the U.S. offering a short-term detox program for PEH using opiates. We'd had several success stories.

Teddy looked at me. "Betty is still clean," he said. "Ernesto, unfortunately, passed away last week."

What?! What?! What?! "Get me his chart, get me his chart!" I shook my head in disbelief. Ernesto was an older, homeless Latino who'd been staying with his family while getting off heroin. He was excited to be clean, so his family would accept him again, and I was happy for him. Homeless opiate users have one of the highest mortality rates, but I tried not to think about that statistic as I treated each of my patients. Instead, I focused on how to keep them alive.

After I finished with Lucia, the next patient was a young woman with multiple abscesses. But she wouldn't let me open them. I gave her antibiotics and told her to come back the following Tuesday. Dixie's social worker called me. Recuperative care had denied her and because she was uninsured, she couldn't go to a nursing home. And she refused to go to a shelter. "We'll taxi her to her usual spot on the streets."

I closed my eyes for a moment then continued.

A few more patients came in. A diabetic entered with an abscess and blood sugar at 399, which is extremely high. We talked about reducing his sugar by avoiding soda and made plans for him to follow up with his regular doctor. The next patient was a young man using heroin to control his chronic pain. I recommended him to a primary care doctor for pain control. In between patients, I thought about

Ernesto. *Did he overdose? Did he have a heart attack?* I called the coroner's office, who told me there was "no cause of death at this time." He had probably started using opiates again and overdosed. Unfortunately, this was the most likely scenario. I thought about Dixie. *Is she any better off now?*

I went to the kitchen to eat my lunch. As I waited for the microwave to *ding*, I saw a familiar face. She had long black hair, piercing blue eyes, and she was holding two star lilies.

"I know you," I said.

She nodded. "I'm Katie. You saved my life five years ago. Happy birthday! I wanted to let you know how much I appreciate all you did for me."

I looked at her, remembering. Five years before, she'd been homeless, pregnant, and a heroin user. But she had come to the clinic for help. At the time, I didn't know how to help her, so I looked online for homes that would take homeless, pregnant drug users. None of them would accept someone on methadone. At that time, most shelters did not practice "harm reduction" and did not allow drug use. Methadone was considered a drug. I knew many patients who had died because of this philosophy. Pregnant women shouldn't detox off opiates because it can cause irreparable harm to the baby and often, preterm labor.

I had to find a way to get Katie methadone and a place to stay that would allow her methadone use. A coworker, Dylan, helped me find a methadone clinic that would treat pregnant women. Then, I called an OB/GYN clinic where I worked in Venice for help finding a shelter that would allow methadone use. Eventually, we found a place in the San Fernando Valley. I saw Katie every week to monitor her methadone use and to make sure she was staying at the shelter. She had the baby and gave it up for adoption.

As we stood in the small kitchen, she told me she'd been clean for five years and had married and regained custody of her older child, an eight-year-old. She'd kept in touch with the parents who had adopted the baby and was volunteering at the Center for Harm Reduction. Almost rendered speechless by how far she had come, I hugged her.

Soon after, Dyhan walked in as I ate my baked ziti. "Tina Marie just came in. She wanted to thank you. She's getting placed at the Georgian."

This was a permanent housing facility. After years of trying to help Tina Marie, with so many people at HHCLA pitching in, she was finally getting permanent—not temporary—housing. Triumph!

Today, Katie is still sober. She works for a homeless agency, leads aerobics, and met her adopted son last year. Triumph!

Over the course of one eventful day, I experienced the tragic devastation of homelessness and rejoiced in the triumphs of concerted efforts to better the lives of PEH. The number of PEH in our great country is astronomical. One-third are severely mentally ill. One half are physically disabled, and one-third are substance users. People experiencing homelessness are ten times more likely to die than their housed counterparts. Opiate users have one of the highest mortality rates. And yet, many can and do recover, with the right interventions. Studies have shown this, and I have experienced it myself, time after time. But working with this incredibly fragile population continually has our heads spinning. Triumphs and tragedies intertwined in a single day—this constant rollercoaster shows the grave situation for each PEH suffering from drug use and/or severe mental illness.

A week after Dixie was returned to the streets, I spoke to her. She told me she'd gotten a second opinion at the Mayo Clinic, and that she didn't need the colonoscopy or a biopsy and her "hemorrhoid" would heal on its own. My colleague saw her a week later, when she'd become too weak to see me at my clinic.

Tragedy.

20

MOURNING THE GENTLE SOULS

ONE LATE MORNING, I WAS SITTING AT A TRENDY CAFE ON Abbott Kinney in Venice, soaking up the warmth of the sun and enjoying the crisp breeze of a perfect Los Angeles winter day, when I received a call. I didn't recognize the number.

"Dr. Susan? This is Kenny's sister," said the voice on the other end.

I had first met Ken ten years before at the Needle Exchange, when he was in his late forties. Over several years, I saw him weekly to tend to the chronic wounds on his legs and arms caused by needle use for heroin. He was Chinese American, and he always wore his long, straight black hair tied back into a ponytail. Over the years, it had become peppered with gray strands. He had gone to college, but sometime afterward, started using drugs.

I had last spoken to Ken about a year before. He had told me he was in a convalescent home. He said he was on dialysis, and they were taking good care of him. I was happy to have heard from him. And now his sister, whom I had never met, was calling.

"How's Ken?" I asked hesitantly, knowing the answer could be something I didn't want to hear.

"That's why I'm calling. I found your number when I was going through his things. I wanted to tell you that he passed away." She paused for a moment. "And I wanted to let you know these past five years were good years for Kenny and my family. I didn't want to let what you did for him go unrecognized."

As a result of using needles, Ken had developed a bone infection in his back, causing the spine to break. On our first meeting, he was bent over in a full bow—his normal stance. Every week, he'd walk slowly into the clinic, his body in the shape of an inverted "L," and wait patiently for his turn. He used a metal walker and hung his belongings—food, clothing—from it in various plastic bags. Like most opioid users, he continued to take heroin to avoid the extreme side effects of withdrawal. And, also like many drug users, he was also using heroin to self-treat the chronic pain that had developed after he broke his back.

His entire lower left leg was an open sore, and I'd spend at least an hour every week debriding the dead tissue and dressing the newly cleaned wounds to promote healing. During these sessions, we'd talk about politics, philosophy, and music. He liked classic rock, so I played it in the background, sometimes breaking out into song with him. One Christmas, he brought me a ceramic tea set. "This is from my mother, for you," he told me. I still use it on special occasions.

Ken lived on the streets of Monterey Park. When I asked about his family, he'd hang his head, saying he didn't want to burden them. He was denied disability not once but twice, and he had no source of income (except for pan handling) and no health care insurance. (This was in the days before expanded Medicaid and Obamacare.)

In 2010, I'd started working for the John Wesley Community Health Institute (JWCH), a Federally Qualified Health Center (FQHC) on Skid Row. It had a program that sought out disabled PEH to provide them with intense case management, including, helping them apply for and get disability. I put Ken on the list, took him to the Salvation Army Shelter in Bell, California, and continued to tend to him at JWCH's satellite clinic there. Once he received disability, he had Medicare and could get medications. I started him on methadone for pain management, which allowed him to stop using heroin. After that, he never used heroin again.

Once he began to receive his disability benefits, he allowed me to call his sister to let her know where he was. Eventually, she took him into her home in the San Fernando Valley. He agreed to the arrangement because he felt he was finally able to contribute something for his care. It was particularly important to him that he wasn't a burden to anyone. Ken followed me to my other community clinic in Hollywood, where I continued to care for him for the next two years.

Those with AIDS, liver failure, kidney failure, and heart failure, along with intravenous heroin users and alcoholics, comprise the most vulnerable homeless group at risk of death. On the practical side of things, a homeless person can cost a community tens of thousands of dollars per year in legal and hospital fees, whereas housing them can reduce costs by almost 60 percent. More importantly, supportive housing allows PEH to rise above survival mode, giving them time and security to work on their health and substance issues. It also gives them the chance to participate in a community, to be purposeful.

Ken was unable to deal with his pain properly, due to lack of medical insurance, so he used heroin, which continually put him at risk for skin infections. The skin infections caused his spinal column infection, which caused vertebral fractures more than once. Eventually, he developed kidney failure. Hospital stays for any one of these conditions would be extremely expensive. Dialysis was the most expensive component of his medical needs. Had he been housed sooner, we may have avoided the hundreds of thousands of dollars in medical bills—but more importantly, he wouldn't have suffered as much.

Some communities are beginning to acknowledge the immense costliness of PEH and are taking steps to invest in better, more proactive care for this at-risk population. And it's working. A 2011–2013 study conducted in Los Angeles showed that supportive housing for the medically and mentally ill homeless decreased the individual cost of hospitalizations and ER visits from $63,808 per year to just $16,913 per year. A 2009 analysis of supportive housing in Los Angeles County found the people with stable housing cost taxpayers 79 percent less than their homeless counterparts, and most of those savings were in healthcare. Green Doors, a nonprofit in Texas, cites that housing PEH decreases the number of emergency room visits by 60 percent. The Economic Roundtable studied pre-and post-housing costs in 2012-13 and found that costs for PEH (medical and legal) reduce from $64,000 to $17,000 after housing. The largest reduction was the elimination of tens of thousands of dollars for facilities at the L.A. County Sheriff Department: mental health jail, medical jail, and hospitalizations. In 2018, the Rand Corporation studied the county's Housing for Health program that provides supportive housing for PEH with high acuity medical issues. After housing 3500 people, 96 percent remained housed for at least a year, and the county saved $6.5 million by the second year of the program. Those who had been housed spent 75 percent less time in the hospital, with 70 percent fewer visits to the ER in the year after moving into supportive housing. The county saved $1.20 for every dollar spent.

These programs are rewarding for doctors, too. I have the privilege to witness the priceless moment when a severely ill person—someone's sister, brother, or parent—finally gets proper care, allowing them to live their tethered life to its fullest. I get to experience what it's like to make a difference in these lives.

For example, I met Betty while doing street outreach in the Skid Row area in August of 2014. She was sleeping on the sidewalk on Sixth Street between San Pedro and St Julien. She was extremely emaciated, and her teeth were completely rotten, which is a sign of chronic methamphetamine or crack cocaine use. Although she was only in her mid-forties, she looked much older.

We were making our street medicine rounds, stopping to ask how people were feeling. Another homeless woman sitting next to Betty on the sidewalk looked up at me and astutely diagnosed, "She needs help."

I leaned down to speak to Betty, but she was groggy and resistant to waking up. I took her blood pressure, which was on the border of being too low. We got her up and walked her to JWCH, the nearest clinic. Later, I found out they knew her well. She had AIDs and had been a patient of the Los Angeles County/USC's satellite HIV clinic, run by my colleague Dr. Jenica Ryu.

Later that day, I spoke to Dr. Ryu. She said that Betty was recently discharged from the hospital after a bout with pneumonia. She'd been extremely sick and had almost died. And before her illness, Betty had rarely shown up for appointments to monitor her HIV and couldn't take HIV medications because of her condition.

The next time we went out for street outreach, I told my partners from the Los Angeles Homeless Services Authority (LAHSA) that we needed to find Betty. We found her sleeping in the courtyard of the Midnight Mission, a nonprofit organization in Skid Row. Betty said she was willing to go to a recuperative care facility, where ill PEH can stay and receive treatment from nursing staff. Once there, she began seeing Dr. Ryu and received HIV medications regularly. She was no longer using crack and had been prescribed psychiatric medications. Betty had also adopted a green-eyed black kitten that lived outside the facility. She fed it daily, and whenever I saw her, she had a big smile. About a year after entering the recuperative care facility, she received supportive housing—her own place but with supportive staff.

When I met her, Betty was at death's door, but because of these organized programs she is living a full life without costing the county so much money. Taking care of a PEH's chronic medical conditions (including mental illness) will always be more cost effective than not addressing them. Win-win!

Despite continual increases in Los Angeles County's homeless population, we're making a difference, one person at a time. The next step in policy changes would be to provide people affordable housing *before* they become homeless, as well as wrap-around services for the severely mentally ill and physically disabled—*before* they become homeless. These types of policies could have helped Betty, or Ken, long before I met them.

"He was a gentle soul," Ken's sister told me on that beautiful, winter morning. I hung up the phone and began to cry, not because he had died, but because of how much this gentle soul had suffered. I thought about the countless nights he had slept on the streets, and the countless days his bent-over body panhandled for change. I recalled many of the suffering souls like Ken and Betty I had met and the countless I hadn't, all of whom are *still* on the streets. I can't wait for the day when I will no longer mourn these gentle souls.

21

LET'S KEEP THE GRAVELY DISABLED OUT OF THE GRAVE

"Dr. Partovi, I got a call from the coroner's office," the outreach nurse from Housing for Health announced on the phone. It was Christmastime, 2015.

"Oh, *fuck*. Who died now?!" When she said the name, I slapped my forehead in despair. For the past several years, we'd had a lot of deaths among chronic drug users in Skid Row: Lena Diggs, Barbara Brown, Tracy Robles, Michael Poore, James Nolan, C.C., Casper (real names). But none of these losses broke my heart more than the loss of Julianne Polniak.

I first met Julianne in July of 2014. She would stand against the wall on the southeast corner of San Julian and Seventh Street. Numerous, mismatched pieces of luggage were chained together and kept next to her makeshift tent. She'd often stand in the sun wearing a black V-neck shirt, a long skirt, and Mary Jane shoes with ribbons tied at her ankles. Julianne's skin was bronzed from both sun and dirt, her hair always pulled back. She was a big girl, tall and wide. On closer look, her shirt was a hospital gown, blackened by soot and tucked into the skirt. She would talk to us, but she never accepted anything—food, soap, a blanket, shelter, or offers of housing or medical care.

"Oh, thank you, but no, thank you. I'm fine. I'll be fine." She was very polite and appreciative of our concern, but always would say the same thing in the end: "My family is coming to get me in 2015." Once it became 2015, she changed it to 2016, etc. The purpose of street medicine is to target the most vulnerable PEH, develop relationships with them, and try to convince them to accept help. It might start with a pair of socks or a toothbrush when your ultimate goal is getting them into permanent, supportive housing. Studies show that housing someone who sleeps on the streets is the best way to begin to treat their medical and psychiatric conditions and addiction. But often, we start slowly, with small goals. One day, about six months after visiting her weekly, Julianne finally allowed me to take her blood pressure! It was 240/120, which is very high. She never let me take it again, and she never came to the clinic two blocks away, although I asked her many times.

When doing my rounds on the streets, the most challenging and heart-breaking folk I come across are the severely mentally ill PEH. They're filthy, pestilent-ridden, and alone. Often, they're resistant to help, sometimes to the point of paranoia. They are the homeless population we can't touch, and so I call them "the untouchables." When considering this vulnerable group, my colleague Anthony Ruffin at Housing Works would lament, "It's more like a death watch now." Instead of asking what we can do for one of these folks, we would ask instead, "Is Joe still alive tonight?"

Why can't we take care of these people? Would you let your mother live on the streets alone, in filth, suffering from serious medical conditions and mental demons?

California's statute on forced psychiatric treatment directs care-takers to involuntarily treat those who are a "danger to self or others," or who are "gravely disabled." Grave disability is defined as "a condition in which a person, as a result of a mental disorder, is unable to provide for his or her basic personal needs for food, clothing OR shelter." That's it. So, when I or Anthony have been watching someone on the streets for months, or even years, and *we* believe that person is at risk of death because they are not capable of taking care of themselves, we may decide to call the Psychiatric Emergency Response Team or the police to come evaluate them. When they arrive, there's no check-off list or formula to use. It's just their opinion. Let's say the emergency team *does* agree the person needs involuntary hospitalization, and "Joe" is taken to the emergency room. Now, it's up to the hospital psychiatrist to decide whether Joe is gravely disabled. If Anthony doesn't show up to explain his observations and experience with Joe, these two profes-sionals can easily disagree at that point. Also, an ER psychiatrist work-ing for a non-county hospital may believe someone to be gravely disabled but is forced to release him if no beds are available. Their opinion on who meets these criteria rises and falls with resource availability.

But let's say that Joe is admitted. If he's been involuntarily hos-pitalized, he's only allowed to stay for seventy-two hours. After that timeframe, if the psychiatrist believes he requires further treatment, they must petition the legal system, and a commissioner will then decide if Joe is gravely disabled. Again, another opinion chiming in. Eventually, the issue of conservatorship may come up, if the person needs someone advocating on his behalf and making his decisions. Then, the patient goes before a judge. A prosecuting attorney will try to explain why Joe is better off having a guardian and a "defending" lawyer tries to convince the judge that the patient has the right to live

how they want. We call that "dying with their rights on." In this scenario, a judge with no medical or psychiatric training has the final
opinion.

If the defense lawyer succeeds in convincing a judge their client
can take care of themselves (and thus, have the right to make decisions
for themselves), then despite all the work the teams have done to stabilize them, they are released back to their usual corner, such as
Seventh and San Julian. Even if they die, they will have died, "with their
rights on."

What if we could interpret grave disability more elaborately and
routinely, with examples, criteria to check-off, and an understanding
of those who are most vulnerable? We need to treat everyone uni-
formly, by referencing established guidelines that specify what grave
disability is, and when it requires long term treatment.

For example, if someone comes to the ER with chest pain, there
is a set of questions to determine whether they are at risk of having a
heart attack. Paramedics, nurses, and doctors all know these questions.
If certain criteria are met, the patient is observed longer in the ER.
There are agreed-upon "best practices" for how to approach chest pain
in a patient. You would never hear, "You may or may not be having a
heart attack, but we have sicker patients already admitted and we just
don't have the room for you." We need a document describing the best
practices for evaluating and treating the gravely disabled so that all
medical professionals can be on the same page, caring for all patients
in an efficient, humane, and fluid process.

A group of experts have started a group called the Grave
Disability Work Group. We agree that lacking insight into the severity
of one's condition is potential for severe illness or death. For example,
Julianne's "I'm fine, I'll be fine." She was at death's door when she said

this! Also, we stress the importance of having a uniform interpretation of grave disability. We need to first reach a consensus about its definition, and then find a way to identify and thus prioritize the most vulnerable.

This includes the concept of "Need to Treat." This means the patient is showing signs that *eventually* will lead to harm. The mental health community knows this requires urgent action. One of my patients, Barbara Brown, died of hypothermia because she wouldn't get out of the cold rain. After hearing the news, I turned to my team member and said, "Julianne is next."

"Yup," she agreed, without hesitation.

We know who's going to die next. Of course, if more people are treated for their psychotic illnesses, we'll need more psychiatric treatment beds and quality, permanent supportive housing that specializes in serving those with severe mental illness. Thus, we need more resources for long-term treatment and care. Let's all agree on who needs to be treated. Then, we can persuade our county and state to allocate money for the mentally ill PEH. At present, resources dedicated to these untouchables are miniscule.

We need to convince politicians that treatment and housing that heals for the SMI is a right. Once it's declared a right, the state will be required to treat and provide housing that heals for all SMI. We will no longer hear "as resources become available." Once this right is guaranteed, we can begin to care for people having acute mental crises, those needing stabilization, and PEH ready to live their best lives in a housing situation that sufficiently addresses their needs.

22

BEHIND THE MUDDIED GLASS

I MET—LET'S CALL HER CARRIE—ON A WEDNESDAY, BUT SHE had no clue what day it was. I was at the Los Angeles County Women's Jail for my first day doing mental health rounds with a team of clinicians and psychologists. I'm a family physician, but I had become the go-to "medical" physician for mental health clinicians when they were worried about their patients potentially having a medical ailment. Because I had spent over seventeen years working with people experiencing homelessness at that point, both in clinics and on the streets, I had extensive experience working with the severely mentally ill. This vulnerable group, especially when they are on the streets, has broken my heart time and time again. Carrie was no different. My heart broke again. I gasped as I looked over at her clinician, who stood at the window next to me.

She nodded. "I know."

Carrie looked like she was in her mid-fifties. She had refused to wear her jail clothes and stood before us naked. She was quite thin, huddled over, and looking out through the muddied glass. But it wasn't mud. She had streaked feces over the glass and on her body. It smelled horrendous.

"Ms. Carrie? Hi. I'm Doctor Partovi. I'm here to say hello and see how you're doing."

She stared at the floor, intently reviewing a make-believe something. "A, B, C," she said. "That goes in A, then you go in B." She remained preoccupied with whatever she saw in front of her.

I tried to get her to acknowledge me. "Ms. Carrie, do you take any medications?"

"Yes, the vitamins go in A, but what about B?"

I noted that she was alert and able to move her body well, but that was about it. The clinician and I returned to our group and the psychologist asked, "That bad?" We both shook our heads as I fought back the tears.

"She's our number one then," the psychologist announced. "Number one" means Carrie would be the first sent to the LA County Jail Psychiatric Hospital when a bed opened up. Luckily, she was transferred later that day. I knew she would get diligent care; it was the only place where they are allowed to medicate and hospitalize involuntarily. Magically, patients often become more "human" after a few days of medication. They may even agree to take the medications on their own.

During the rest of the rounds, I would compare everyone to Carrie. Some would yell at me, which was reassuring because it showed some engagement with the outside world, and some would gladly talk to me. I felt reassured that no one seemed as bad as Carrie; she was still number one. But I kept asking myself how she had ended up in prison. I couldn't believe she was a serious criminal, or that she posed a threat to others. For all the time I made mental health rounds at the LA County Women's Jail, I had never inquired why any inmate was there.

For me, it was easy to see how Carrie had ended up in jail. Had I not intervened, my sister Michelle would have certainly ended up in jail. She had been on the road to a similar outcome. Once a competent high school French teacher, she started behaving strangely in her early fifties. She stopped keeping her house orderly, and she wouldn't bathe or take her medications. She wandered around the neighborhood, entering homes without consent, and walked to the grocery store in 100+ temperatures. As her ability to care for herself slowly deteriorated, neighbors often called the police on her. Finally, she was diagnosed with frontal temporal lobe dementia, a genetic disease that causes atrophy of the frontal lobe of the brain (controls behavior and personality) and the temporal lobes (language and memory). I found part-time and then, full-time caretakers, and eventually, a locked nursing home. Six years later, Michelle was like an infant, unable to speak or understand much. She required psychiatric medications to keep her behavior in check. Had I not stepped in, I believe she could have ended up like Carrie—homeless, in jail, or worse.

Carrie's story is not about the horrible treatment of the mentally ill in jail; on the contrary, I was impressed with how caring the guards and the mental health clinicians were with that population. Everyone knew these severely ill people didn't belong there, and most people interacting with this group tried to make it as easy as possible for them. Still, it was jail, and inmates were placed in cells. This isolation and confinement can be the perfect storm for someone who normally can't deal with daily life, causing them to explode into their full, psychotic self. So, why is Carrie (and 20 percent of the LA County jail population who are mentally ill) in jail and not at home with loved ones, or in a facility where they can eat, dress, and enjoy life with the support of professional caretakers?

In the case of Michelle, I ended up spending about five thousand dollars a month for her caretakers in Lancaster. Plus, I was paying her rent, utilities, and other bills. Not many people can sustain that type of extra expense, and I was no exception. Eventually, I moved her in with my mom, who already had 24/7 care for her dementia. Fortunately, my mom had a pension I used to pay for her caretakers and bills. My sister, however, had cashed out all her benefits when she was fired from the school district. I applied for In Home Services through Medicaid, which paid for two days a week. It was less expensive for me but still required out-of-pocket costs. Did Carrie have a sister? A daughter? Most severely mentally ill have ostracized themselves from family, after becoming incredibly difficult to handle and possibly, refusing help for a long time. Sometimes, families find it too expensive and exasperating to care for someone like Michelle or Carrie. Or maybe Carrie truly had no family.

So, who takes care of Carrie? Right now, taxpayers do. It costs $178 a day for Carrie to be in jail ($65,000 a year, according to Justice LA), three times the cost of caring for an inmate with no mental illness. This is a waste of money and doesn't provide the best care for people like Carrie. In fact, it costs about $25,000 per year for a permanent housing situation with significant support. The goal is that after hospitalization, Carrie would continue to take medications, become more coherent and be able to have some semblance of a normal, functioning life. The county has programs that can divert people like Carrie into full-time care, which is what she needs. But why didn't this happen before she landed in jail? Why didn't we take care of her before she spiraled out of control, and before we spent tens of thousands of dollars on legal fees, court fees, custody overtime, psychiatry, psychology, clinicians, a hospital, and me?

The answer is deinstitutionalization of the severely mentally ill. In the United States, institutionalization began in the mid-1800s as a result of the reform movement led by Dorothea Hicks, an advocate for the mentally ill. After experiencing the conditions for mentally ill prisoners in East Cambridge, Massachusetts, Hicks dreamt of providing humane care for those who couldn't care for themselves. It was the era of "moral treatment." However, as the hospitals became overwhelmed with patients, they became human warehouses, with anything but humane care. Up to the 1940s, many hospitalized patients were severely neglected and even abused. At that time, a national movement for reform ensued, but instead, hospitals began to close, leaving nowhere for patients to go.

In the 1960s, "liberating" the mentally ill became a part of the Civil Rights Movement. In 1967, the LPS (Letterman/Petis/Short) Act of California restricted involuntary commitment based solely on "danger to self and others" and grave disability—which, at the time, was defined as being unable to provide oneself with food, clothing, or shelter. "Need to treat" based on mental or medical deterioration or eventual harm to self was off the table. The American Association of Psychiatry had said that when someone is deteriorating psychiatrically, urgent action is required. They called this "need to treat." However, we don't look at behavior. We only ask if the person can provide food, clothing, or shelter for themselves. The rest of the states soon followed suit. This was the beginning of allowing people like Carrie or Michelle to "die with their rights on."

Other influences against institutionalization arose from political and cultural realms. (e.g., psychology became synonymous with

Freud's sexual promiscuity; caring for people in institutions was linked to communism; less government involvement was deemed best, etc.). The most substantial cause of deinstitutionalization, however, has been an economic one.

In 1965, Medicaid was enacted. This federal money was intended to help states and local communities with the acute medical costs for low-income individuals. However, the states decided to shift their mental health costs to Medicaid, which would only pay medical hospitals (not state mental hospitals) and skilled nursing homes. Also, Medicaid won't cover more than three days of psychiatric care, so hospitals tend to discharge patients inappropriately—before they are ready and without a follow-up plan. Skilled nursing homes aren't staffed with the expertise needed for this population, and they can often pick and choose who is accepted. They don't want difficult patients! Even if an intense outpatient treatment center has been proven effective, it's not covered by Medicaid.

As a result, the number of mentally ill PEH skyrocketed, and the number of mentally ill incarcerated soared. Over the past several decades, the number of mentally ill in prison inversely correlated with the decrease in the number of mental institution beds.

As a society, we have been brainwashed into thinking that Carrie, while experiencing full, untreated psychosis, has the right to make decisions on her own. If she doesn't want help, we should honor her desire to be independent. We have been convinced to believe that Carrie *wants* to be homeless, suffering from paranoia and hallucinations, naked in a cold cell using feces as an art vehicle. We have been brainwashed into thinking this way, so we don't have to pay for Carrie's care. It really boils down to money. Yet, there's an astounding secret: It costs more money to care for those on the streets than to provide the humane care they deserve. In fact, it can cost up to $100,000 in medical and legal costs per year to care for a homeless person. The majority of PEH suffer from medical and psychiatric ailments. Studies show that those who live on the street are ten times more likely to die. But before they die, they spend a lot of time in emergency rooms and hospitals. Furthermore, those with severe mental illness and chronic medical conditions and those who use drugs are most vulnerable for death. Often, we hear "There isn't a bed for Carrie. No one will pay for it." But we never hear there isn't a jail bed for her. Why do we never have hospital beds available, but never run out of jail beds?

So, what is the answer to the tragic and chaotic result of deinstitutionalization? I AM NOT advocating that we lock up and hospitalize all mentally ill PEH. But I am advocating for intensive care for those I call the "super-dupers," the severely mentally ill and incapacitated living on the streets. These folks might sit on the same urine and feces-stained sidewalk for years, surrounded by loads of junk. Or they might wander through the neighborhoods without any belongings, barefoot and disheveled, talking to people who aren't there. Aggressive medication is the first step. Modern psychiatric medications work amazingly well. Patients have a variety of options; if they don't like one, they can try another, until one works

Some mentally ill people need to be conserved, meaning, someone needs to care for them and make important decisions for them. Though I am not my sister Michelle's legal guardian, she allows me to care for her and make decisions for her. From the very beginning of her struggles, I initiated getting a power of attorney for financial and health care decisions. Again, having a conservator doesn't mean getting "locked up" in a mental institution, as it's portrayed sometimes in the movies. It can mean living with loved ones or in a Board and Care or assisted living. These facilities have 24/7 staff and usually, nursing.

Patients tend to be more mobile and can care for basic needs like feeding and bathing themselves. But even with a conservator, some can even live on their own with daily support. Some mentally ill do need to be in a long-term, locked facility, if it's determined they are incapable of keeping themselves out of harm's way.

But first, we need a smooth process established for caring for this population. We all need to be on the same page about what is best for Carrie. We know she is gravely disabled because if left to her own devices, she would not be able to provide food, clothing, or shelter for herself. Would she be able to provide life-sustaining, unspoiled food, and potable water for herself? Would she be able to provide clothing suitable for the weather? Would she be able to provide and sustain safe shelter for herself? I doubt it. This is the California legal definition of grave disability. Then, we would look at her history and present the evidence in court that she cannot care for herself.

Furthermore, the definition of grave disability needs to include severe deterioration of mental and/or medical health, not just being able to provide food, clothing, and shelter for oneself. And, most importantly, we need hospital beds for people like Carrie, not jail beds! The entire county of Los Angeles only has about one thousand beds available for emergent psychiatric hospitalization and around another one thousand beds, if needed for further psychiatric stabilization. Furthermore, we only have a few hundred beds at Board and Cares. There isn't anywhere for these patients to go if they require advanced care. Let's invest in taking care of Carrie by investing in an appropriate housing situation for her.

If I had seen Carrie in the streets, covered in feces, suffering hallucinations, and exposed to the weather, infestations, and illness, it would be near impossible to hospitalize her against her will for the time required for stabilization and, eventually, housing that would suit her needs. But if she had stolen a bag of chips, or trespassed, or committed some other small offense, there would always be a bed for her in one of California's jails.

23

MENTAL ILLNESS, METH, AND SKID ROW: MAKING IT HAPPEN

First Attempt

"I'M YOUR NEW ASSISTANT," PATTY ANNOUNCED ONE DAY AS I came into Homeless Health Care Los Angeles's (HHCLA) Needle Exchange. She was short, bubbly, soft-spoken, and caring. It was 2006, and I had been working on Skid Row for two years already. I was "the doc" who saw heroin injection users with medical needs. With the emersion of community-acquired MRSA (Methicillin-resistant Staphylococcus aureus, the type of staph infection that is difficult to treat because of resistance to some antibiotics and is often caused from using needles to inject drugs), each week I treated scores of skin infections and chronic wounds. While at HHCLA, I learned how to teach safe injection use and further developed my thoughts about how to care for people experiencing homelessness, beginning with accepting my patients for who and where they were.

Patty quickly became skilled in this environment, too. She could anticipate my needs during procedures, and we worked well together.

As we came to know each other better, she told me her story. She had used crack and been homeless, she said. It was hard for me to imagine this plump, bashful woman as a hard-core drug user. We talked about her life and her kids, especially her son, who was having anger issues in school. She was striving to have a "normal" life and do right by her kids. The first step: a good job!

Spending our days working with the most difficult patient population formed a bond between us. Like war buddies. One day, we saw one of our regulars for scabies, again. Because of the unsanitary conditions on the street, he kept coming back with it, so we took matters into our own hands. We stripped him down, and Patty and I slathered anti-scabies cream all over his body. His hair was long and stringy, his body skin and bones.

"You look like a wet puppy," Patty exclaimed, which made us all laugh.

Another day, we saw a patient with a foot infection. He was a diabetic but couldn't afford his medications. He was crying because he was in so much pain. The reason became shockingly obvious when he took his shoe off.

"Quick, Patty," I said. "Get me a basin with water and Betadine."

She hurried to follow my orders. We managed to place his disintegrating foot, swarming with maggots, into the tub before Patty ran out of the clinic with her hand over her mouth. In the restroom, she threw up. War buddies!

In 2008, HHCLA could no longer afford a medical assistant, and Patty was let go. For six years, I lost track of her, but one day in 2014, I was at the VOA (Volunteers of America) starting my street medicine program on Skid Row with Los Angeles County's Department of Health Services (DHS), when I saw her again.

"Hi Doctor Partovi!" she called out. I was surprised to see her. She was the same cute, bubbly woman, and seemed to be in good spirits.

"We're rehearsing for a play," she said. "I messed up, but I'm back on track and doing good!"

At that time, it was still difficult for me to understand what "messing up" looked like for her. She still looked well if a bit thinner. It worried me that she lived on Skid Row, even though she was housed.

More time went by. In 2016, I started working in the women's Los Angeles County jail once DHS took over. One day, a guard told me Patty wanted me to know she was there, as an inmate. She was too embarrassed to see me, he said. My heart sank, knowing she must have been using again.

I didn't see her again until 2018. It was a typical busy day at the Needle Exchange, which by then was called the Center for Harm Reduction. I had two family medicine residents rotating with me, and several pre-med helpers assisting. When I heard a commotion outside, I went to see what was happening. Across the street, a skinny and disheveled woman was trying to push a stroller missing a wheel, crammed with stuff, as she cussed out a man on my side of the street.

"Give me back my things, you fucking thief! I used to work here! I'll kill you, motherfucker. You stole my shit!"

The man looked at me. "You better get this bitch out of my face, or I'll kill her."

"Just walk away," I pleaded. "Pay her no mind."

My co-worker said, "Dr. Partovi, that's Patty."

I was shocked. I didn't recognize her. She was so thin, a complete mess. Her hair was matted and her clothes worn, but it was her face that struck me. She looked like a completely different person; her face contorted with anger. I had never heard her cuss before. The only way I knew it was her was because of the unique mole she had.

"Patty, get out of the street," I said. "Come with me." She continued ranting, and I continued pleading with the guy to back off. "Let's catch up, Patty," I said. "Come inside!"

Finally, she acquiesced.

Once we got inside the clinic, I sat her down. I wasn't sure how to start the conversation. "Patty," I said. "What's going on?"

"People keep taking my shit! Spirits are everywhere, messing with my head." She started to cry. "He looks like my son!" she said, glancing at one of the residents.

I noticed patches where her hair was missing; she continually rubbed her head.

She began to talk about different voices she heard, and about spirits and electric connections. I gave her a prescription for medication to help with the voices. I found out she was now using meth, the new scourge of the community. Meth is known to cause acute psychosis, and long-term use could cause chronic psychosis similar to the symptoms seen with schizophrenia.

"Come here every week," I told Patty. "We'll take care of you."

She nodded. "Okay, Dr. Partovi. I only trust you."

After she left, I immediately started loudly weeping. I'm a fairly private person and rarely show emotion—especially in the workplace. One of my co-workers hugged me as I continued to sob. I felt so impotent; she was a shadow of the competent person I once knew. *Should I take her home with me?* I entertained a variety of thoughts. *She's too unstable. I can't trust her with my animals. What if she thinks one of them is an evil spirit and hurts them?"*

I told Mark, the CEO of HHCLA, what had happened. "We have to help her," he said. "She's one of us." I knew his heart would break over her condition, as mine had. I also knew he'd have my back and be prepared to do whatever it took to get her safely off the streets.

I called my connection with mental health outreach, who said he'd help. But like most drug users on Skid Row, Patty was hard to keep track of. Occasionally, she'd come into the Needle Exchange. I gave her samples of the psychiatric medication, which she agreed to take but then would admit she hadn't. She was in and out of jail and the psych ward—the oh-so-common, revolving doors for those who are experiencing homelessness with mental health and/or drug issues.

One day, Ben Oreskes from the *Los Angeles Times* called me. We had met before during a town hall meeting on homelessness. "I wrote a story about this homeless woman the other day," he said. "After it ran, her daughter reached out. She hadn't seen her mother in four years. The mother's name is Patty Jones. I'm trying to find her to bring them together. Do you know her?" He was shocked to hear how I knew her and reiterated the importance of their reconciliation.

I alerted my staff to call Ben if she turned up, and the next week, she did. Patty was extremely gregarious that day, cracking jokes and talking about the electric connections she had in her body. I asked her if it was okay to call Ben, and she said yes. He was interviewing Ben Carson at the time and couldn't get away.

The following week, David, one of our long-time staff members, suddenly passed away. The team at HHCLA met that Friday to grieve as a family. We shared stories, and someone reminded us about what David would always say when facing a difficulty: "Make it happen. Just make it happen." And I thought, that's really the philosophy of HHCLA and mine, as well. "Make it Happen!"

After lunch, Ben called again. "Dr. Partovi, I'm here at the Refresh Spot with Patty. She's having a hard time."

"I'll be right there," I told him.

The Refresh Spot in Skid Row provides shower and laundry services. It's run by HHCLA under the direction of one of my long-time colleagues, Evans, who knew Patty from back in the day. When I arrived, Patty and Ben were sitting in a corner fenced off by a chain. She was holding a metal rod. She was in one of her angry moods, accusing and threatening anyone who tried to engage her. I sat down next to her.

"I gotta get off the streets, Dr. Partovi," she said. "I keep getting attacked."

I looked at Evans. "Let's make it happen!"

He nodded in agreement.

Later, Evans called the Sobering Center, a place where PEH can spend a night or two if they're too drunk or high to stay safe. He obtained approval, but she wouldn't go.

"I need to be by myself," Patty said.

I called Joanne, one of our directors at HHCLA, who told me we might be able to use money from the Wiggins grant, which provided money for interim housing, specifically for those living on the streets of Skid Row.

"But call Cesar," she told me. "He's in charge of housing."

Evans called Maggie, another director, who spoke with Mark, our CEO, who agreed and said he'd cut a check.

Cesar called one of his "brothers" about housing. "Call Peter," he told me. "He has a motel."

I called Peter and got the address.

We loaded all of Patty's belongings into my SUV, after coaxing her with a McDonalds run. But first we had to "get her things" at the tent down the street. There were people lined up outside this tent, and I suspected what she was really getting was some meth to take with her. She spent a good fifteen minutes in this tent.

We drove forty minutes to Baldwin Hills. I put the charge for the room on my card knowing I'd be reimbursed, but to be honest, I would have footed the bill as part of my new declaration to "Make it Happen." Often when talking about homelessness, I return to a basic common sentiment: *I would never allow my sister or mom to live on the streets.* When I do this, decisions are usually simple.

Before we reached the hotel, we took Patty to the grocery store as I called in a prescription for her antipsychotic medication to the pharmacy next door. Ben had to leave so I was alone with Patty, who was now acting a little manic. She picked things from the shelves and ran ahead of me. I felt like I was shopping with a toddler who wasn't particularly good at listening! She kept escaping to find more items to place in the cart. As we checked out, she tried to get liquor from the locked cabinet, but I shook my head at the checker. Patty started yelling at one of the clerks. I waved my hands behind her to let him know not to pay her any mind, and he disengaged.

Somewhere, Patty found a piece of foil and pressed it against her forehead. "Gotta keep the spirits away!" Then she started yelling. "She's my doctor! I know her. I trust her." She was speaking into the air, to nonexistent beings.

I finally got her out of the store, and when we picked up her psychosis medication next door, I made sure she took it. When we finally reached the motel, a small place with about ten rooms and a few cars parked out front, I helped put away her things. It was a basic room: bed, television, some faded pictures on the wall and a small refrigerator. As I was leaving, she disconnected all the plugs and used a lighter to ward off spirits in every corner. She chanted something unintelligible, keeping a piece of foil near her forehead.

I hesitated in the doorway, certain she would leave—or burn the place down. "I'll see you tomorrow," I said, taking one last look around.

The next day, I showed up before my evening, urgent care shift, around two in the afternoon. I had brought some clean clothes and underwear. Patty was still there! She had been sleeping! I ensured that she took her medication, and we walked to the corner market for cigarettes. I knew not to give her money, but I'd buy whatever she wanted, mostly.

On day three, Ben went to visit. He called me from her room. "She's still here." We were both surprised. At my request, he watched her take her medications.

I visited her on day four, and she was still there. I asked her if she was still using.

She laughed. "I don't have any money."

"Do you hear voices?" I asked.

"No."

On day five, Ben arranged to pick up Patty's daughters in San Bernardino and I picked Patty up and brought her to Homeless Health Care LA's main site in Echo Park. We met with Allie, who oversaw our outpatient drug treatment program, about getting Patty back in. We met with Cesar about temporary housing. Patty received a bus pass and a voucher to get ID. Mark, our CEO, came down and gave her a big hug.

Eventually, Ben and Patty's daughters showed up. It was quite a joyous occasion. We went to a local café for lunch as the three caught up. At one point Patty told one of her daughters to try her pineapple cake.

"I don't like cooked fruit," the young woman said. She was tiny like Patty and looked like a teenager, although I knew she was in her late twenties.

"Just try it!"

"Oh, Mom!" She sounded like a frustrated teenager, like no time had passed at all. They showed Patty pictures of her grandkids and giggled all through the lunch. It was sweet. No one asked, "Where have you been? Why are you using drugs? Why haven't you called us?" They just enjoyed being in each other's presence.

Earlier on the drive there, I had asked Patty what had happened to restart her habit, after so many years.

"My mom was killed by a drunk driver in 2015. I was living at the Lamp House (housing for those with mental health issues, then next door to the Refresh Spot), but I started using again. I was there for seven months and then got housing at the Boyd. I was there for a year and a half until I was kicked out. I wasn't following the rules. I've been on the streets ever since."

This is a common scenario. Many people who attain housing get clean. Unfortunately, when trauma occurs, their limited coping skills cause them to return to what they know best, getting numb.

As we were leaving, Patty asked her daughter for money. She gave her twenty dollars. Normally, this is a very innocent act—a family member trying to do good for another. In this case, I knew the potential outcome. After we got back into my car, I turned to Patty. "I know it's none of my business," I said, "but what are you going to do with the twenty dollars?"

"Yeah, I saw your face when she gave it to me." She looked out the window. "You can drop me off at the train. I know how to get back."

"Are you sure?"

"Yeah, there's a bus stop right there."

And before I could object, she got out of the car. "I'll call you when I get to the hotel," she said.

I never heard from her. I went to the hotel the next day. She wasn't there and hadn't slept in her bed. Her daughter texted me to ask how her mom was doing. I decided to give Patty one more day and didn't answer immediately, in case there was no cause for worry.

Ben and I met at the hotel. She still hadn't been there. We packed up her things and put them into my car. We gave the unused food to the next occupant, who was waiting with a People Assisting the Homeless (PATH) worker for the now-available room. She, too, was homeless, hoping to temporarily get off the streets. When we told the PATH worker, a fellow "war buddy," about Patty, she said she recognized the scenario quite well. "It's part of the process," she said.

When dealing with those battling addiction, unless there is constant support, it's difficult for them to stay clean. The addiction is too strong to overcome. They often abandon all progress for another chance to get high. It's not a choice; it's an addiction that often takes over all common sense. It's pure brain chemistry. Many times, the addiction wins. But we don't give up on them. We keep at it until something sticks.

I was speaking to a co-worker recently. She is a drug counselor now for Homeless Health Care Los Angeles. She told me she had used cocaine and lived on the streets for seven years. I was flabbergasted that this very capable, caring woman who handles scores of clients at a time had once been homeless. Seven years! "That's like a lifetime!" I said to her. "Yes," she calmly answered. "What was the clincher—what got you off the streets?" I asked. She said, "I was arrested, so instead of going to prison, I chose a drug treatment program. I had been in programs before, but this time told myself, 'This is it. I'm gonna get clean!'" I asked what had made her stick to the program. "Nothing," she said. "I decided I was going to work the program the right way. I got a sponsor and worked the steps. When you work the steps every day, over time, your brain gets used to being sober." Brain chemistry!

I finally told Patty's daughter what had happened. I told her we wouldn't give up. And we won't. This is what it takes to work with the traumatized mentally ill and those who self-treat with drugs. A team of caring individuals must work together toward a common goal, treating each person with respect, compassion, understanding, and full acceptance. The ultimate goal is housing the individual while providing the support that allows them to get better, succeed, and thrive. I told my colleagues to keep an eye out for Patty and that we'd try again. We all know the mantra. Somehow, we will make it happen. We won't give up on Patty or anyone like her.

Marinating

Over the next few months, I placed Patty into a series of motels paid for by Homeless Health Care LA, while waiting for her to get into interim housing. She stayed in one for four weeks but eventually was kicked out for damaging the television and having inconsiderate visitors who made noise at all hours. She tracked me down again, and I put her back at the original hotel. I didn't give her any antipsychotics this time (due to me being too tired and thinking naively if she wasn't using, maybe she wouldn't act out). Five days later, I received a call from the manager saying she was "crazy." He didn't speak English very well, and I didn't take the time to try to understand what he was saying. The next day he called me again, saying she had to leave. I told him I would pick Patty up the next morning.

When I arrived, the door was open. The bed and bed frame were overturned, and trash was everywhere. The television was shattered, the pictures removed from the walls and destroyed, and the bedding was thrown onto the floor. It was a disaster zone, and she was a mess.

Patty looked up from where she sat on the floor. "Dr. Partovi," she said. "This place is filthy. There's feces inside the walls. There are sensors and cameras detecting my every move." She started to cry hysterically. "They're raping me," she added.

I tried to calm her down as I began to clean up. I didn't know what else to do. When I had checked in at the office, the manager said he hadn't slept in two nights because Patty had been pacing non-stop and bothering the other residents.

I realized if I took Patty back to Skid Row in her current condition, she would get beaten up or worse. She had proven she could not sustain shelter for herself. Thus, we should be allowed to hospitalize her against her will. After working on the streets of Los Angeles County for so many years, I had learned how difficult it was to hospitalize someone against their will—even if they did meet the criteria. This is mostly because of the lack of options for long-term psychiatric care. Neither Medicaid nor Medicare cover the cost, and there is no funding to care for our brothers and sisters suffering from chronic, severe mental illness. And so, they stay on the streets suffering from their demons, vulnerable to potential violence, further psychiatric decay and disease, and at risk of rotating in and out of jail.

As I continued to clean up Patty's motel room, I tried to reason with her. "Look," I said. "You're having a hard time. Let's go to the hospital so we can talk to someone."

"I'm not going to the hospital!" She continued to yell at people who weren't there.

Finally, I stopped and looked her in the eye. "Patty, this is your choice. You come with me to the hospital, or I call the police."

"I'm not going to the hospital!" Her energy grew angrier. She began pacing around the room.

I called 911. Now, why did I call the police? The LA County Department of Mental Health does have a Psychiatric Mobile Response Team (PMRT) that I could have called. However, in my experience, they could take hours to respond. As I watched Patty get more and more agitated, I felt I didn't have that kind of time. Also, the PMRT often didn't agree with my definition of grave disability. So, I called the police because she was escalating, and I didn't know what to do. The dispatcher must have asked me five times if she had a weapon, and I assured them over and over that she didn't.

Fifteen minutes later, LAPD officers calmly and cautiously approached the open motel room door. Patty saw them right away.

"You're not in trouble," they told her. "We just want to talk to you and check in."

She began to calm down and started telling one officer about the feces, being raped, demons, etc., while the other officer talked to me. I tried to explain Patty's story and why I thought she was gravely disabled and potentially a danger to self. I explained how pugnacious she was and that I thought she could easily provoke someone into harming her. The officer listened to what I had to say and was sympathetic. I knew she had to call the Mental Evaluation Unit, the highly trained officers who make decisions about whom can be placed on a hold. I also knew they wouldn't think she met the criteria, and when the officer called, they didn't. I thanked the officers for being so kind and caring, and for helping to calm her down. Most of the police I have met in working with people experiencing homelessness and the mentally ill are exceptionally skilled and truly caring. But they're not mental health experts.

I finished cleaning and put the rest of Patty's things into my car. I apologized multiple times to the manager and once we were in the car, I decided to turn right instead of left. I decided to take her to Harbor-UCLA's emergency room, where they have a psychiatric emergency department and inpatient hospital. I put on my county badge and told Patty we were going to talk to a doctor. I was dreading the moment when I'd run up against the one person at the hospital who wouldn't agree with my assessment. This invariably happened.

The ER nurse practitioner met me. She listened as I told her why Patty and I were there.

She listened calmly and spoke when I had finished. "She has to get tested for COVID-19 first."

Okay, first hurdle. A tall, dark-haired nurse named Mike met us. I told him Patty's story, hoping to get as many allies on my side as possible. Patty started dancing and laughing, not making much sense.

Administering the test was a challenge. We tried explaining to her how to do it, and we tried telling her to let me do it. She really was like a toddler, so eventually I held her down and Mike got the swab in her nose. I was not letting a friggin Q-tip keep Patty from getting the care she needed. We waited three hours for the results in a private room in the ER. For two of those hours, she was yelling and screaming at people who weren't there and intermittently sobbing uncontrollably. I asked Mike to call the ER doc to ask if we could give her something to calm down. I again told her story to the ER resident, who was truly kind and understanding.

"Patty, do you want to take something to help relax?" I asked.

"No, I have to keep my wits about me," she retorted. But then she said, "I'll take the medicine you normally give me."

Eagerly, I looked at the resident. Knowing they wouldn't have that medicine in the ER, I asked, "How about something similar?"

In twenty minutes, Big Mike brought in the medications. At first, Patty was reluctant, but then she took them. Within a half hour, she was curled up on the bed, sleeping soundly. Eventually, the Covid-19 test came back negative, and we walked our now-sleepy girl to the Psychiatry ER, a separate area for mentally ill patients, where they told me she curled up on another bed and continued to sleep. I wasn't allowed in there, but the nurse eventually came out. This time, I told Patty's story with more emphasis, again trying to get buy-in from the psych nurse. She listened without interruptions and seemed caring. She went back into the psychiatry ER and eventually, came out with the psychiatry resident. This was it. I was ready to give it my all. I practiced many times. I told him that I had spent seventeen years working with people experiencing homelessness and mental health issues. I relayed that I had been studying the California laws on what qualifies for a hold. I said she was at risk of harming herself and gravely disabled because—

"Oh, yeah. We're putting her on a hold," the resident interrupted. "She is gravely disabled."

I almost started to cry. He'd agreed. I knew more hurdles were ahead, but at least we had time now to get Patty stabilized and start looking for a place for her to go afterwards.

While we had been waiting for the Covid-19 test to come back, I had emailed La Tina Jackson, head of the Full-Service Partnership Program (FSP) at LA County's Department of Mental Health (DMH). We had worked together before, and I knew she was very responsive and caring now.

Later that week while Patty was still hospitalized, La Tina put me in touch with the SPA 4 director (L.A. has eight service provider areas (SPA), who then introduced me to Victoria, the director at Portals, a Department of Mental Health agency downtown. I spoke with Victoria that Friday, and she promised to work on finding a place for Patty. One of her workers called me on Saturday asking for more details. The plan was to interview Patty on Monday to enroll her into the program. Another hurdle I was trying to postpone thinking about was that we needed Patty's agreement to get her in the program.

On Friday, I emailed the chair of the psychiatry department at Harbor-UCLA, a colleague of mine. When he called me, I told him about Patty and her story. He reassured me that he'd make sure she wasn't released until she was stable, and a good discharge plan was in place. I expressed my gratitude for the help from him and all the residents I had met since taking care of Patty there. On Monday, the new psychiatry ER resident called me. Again, I told Patty's story. She agreed to keep Patty there until her housing situation was arranged. Another person truly understood the repercussions of releasing someone who can't take care of themselves back on the streets, and this fact almost moved me to tears. "I'm putting her on a two-week hold," she said before we hung up.

I called the social worker and Victoria at Portals, leaving it in their hands to work on the housing situation. Finally, I had some peace of mind.

The next day, I received a call from the inpatient psych resident (on the psychiatric floor) asking about Patty. She had just rotated in and wanted a briefing. After I finished, she said, "Okay, we're going to let her marinate here for a while."

What a great metaphor. People experiencing acute psychosis often calm down within seventy-two hours (the length of a first "hold") but really, their brain chemistry needs more time to stabilize. Two weeks is a good start, but many need months to stabilize. It doesn't mean they have to be in a locked facility for that length of time, but they do need major support.

The following week, Patty called me from the hospital. Her mood was cheerful. She asked for her daughter's phone number, complained that they wouldn't let her smoke, and asked me to bring snacks because she wasn't getting enough to eat. Also, she said getting the long-acting shot for her psychosis might be a good idea. *Progress!* She said she wanted to leave but also understood the need to get housing before her release.

"We want to keep you safe," I told her.

"Yes, Dr. Partovi," she said. "I understand."

She was starting to sound like her old self, reasonable and upbeat. I knew what it was like to have a loved one with psychosis, needing both acute and long-term care. One difference in my experience with my sister (not the case with most psychiatric patients) was that everyone was willing to communicate with me. Most of the time, family members are left in the dark regarding the care plan; often, the patient is discharged without family being notified.

One of the most crucial elements of a successful care plan for someone suffering from psychosis is having a loved one take part as an advocate. In Patty's case, I knew many of the pieces of the puzzle and thus, was able to paint the complete picture to other care providers, and to share what other resources were in play. California's privacy laws do not prohibit family member involvement (unless implicitly stated by the patient), but they do leave the final say to the mental health provider. And so, family members are rarely contacted for important details, or take part in the conversation about care. For a successful treatment plan and outcome, having a loved one involved is key. For Patty, I acted as the loved one and this was a first, positive part of her care.

Second, every provider I encountered was extremely empathetic to Patty's case and used common sense (which is supported by the law) to do what was best for her chance to live a healthy life.

Third, the doctors followed the law. They heard her case and determined that she met the criteria for grave disability, without being influenced by the shortage of long-term care facilities.

Fourth, police can be very caring and helpful with potentially violent people suffering from psychosis, but they are not the best choice for assessment. As soon as possible, a mental health expert should assess and help with the situation.

Fifth: We need a funding stream for long-term psychiatric care, in order to provide better stabilization. If I were hit by a car and suffered a spinal cord injury, Medicaid would pay for the hospitalization AND the months of rehabilitation needed, post-hospitalization. Why don't they pay for psychiatric rehabilitation? This seems discriminatory to me. Furthermore, we need to beef up our board and care facilities. So many have shut down due to lack of funding.

Sixth: Drug users often have severe mental disturbances. It doesn't matter which came first; the mental disturbance needs to be addressed first. Then, we can deal with the drug issue.

Seventh: We need to adequately address drug use. We need to have patience, not expecting that people will get clean on the first try. Furthermore, we need to be okay with small improvements over time and not demand immediate sobriety in order to receive resources. In fact, studies show that housing people who use drugs with support will improve their lives all around, including decreasing or stopping drug use.

All of this takes time, energy, collaboration, and cooperation. This is how we start making a dent in the homeless numbers in both Los Angeles County and the entire United States.

Patty stayed in the hospital for ten days. On a Tuesday morning, she was discharged and sent to a hotel through Project Room Key in Century City. This was L.A. County's attempt to house PEH using unused hotels during the Covid-19 pandemic. A brilliant idea! She left the hotel Wednesday after breakfast and headed downtown. She missed the FSP worker who came to see her, and she missed the 7:00 p.m. curfew. On Thursday, she came to the Center for Harm Reduction, asking me to place her in another hotel. I said she had to go back to that one. I tried to convince her to take the long-acting injectable medication, reminding her that at one point, she'd thought it was a good idea. I called the hotel and spoke to the manger, who told me she could return.

I called the FSP worker, who came down. But Patty had left before we could take her back to the hotel. She denied that she was psychotic when I tried to convince her to take the medication.

"I just had emotional issues," she explained. "I think the demons have brought you to their side."

In retrospect, a board and care may have been more appropriate. Patty lacked insight into her condition, making it difficult to adhere to her life-saving treatment. She needed to be in a facility she wouldn't be able to leave so easily, for a longer time period. Perhaps some kind of step down facility where they could keep an eye on her, engage her in activities, allow her to smoke and eat what she wanted and connect with her family, address her drug use, and keep her safe. To be honest, I'm not sure if this type of high-level community care facility exists but how great would it be if it did! Some would ask, again, who would pay for this? And yet, no one ever asks who pays when she goes to jail or gets hospitalized repeatedly. This costs the county much more than if we had such a utopia. Some believe Patty has the right to refuse treatment, even if she doesn't quite understand that the refusal results in constant suffering from her demons and the increased risk of dying and incarceration. *Yeah, that's the more humane thing to do.*

"Meds First, Housing Second"

After Patty had left the Center for Harm Reduction that Thursday, I hadn't seen her in weeks. I made the difficult decision that if she came to me for help, I would only put her into a hotel if she agreed to the long-acting injection version of the antipsychotic she had been trying to take orally. I really struggled with this decision. *Am I manipulating her into taking medication? Am I using the human rights need of housing as a carrot, to persuade her into taking her medications?* No. The only way she would stay in a hotel without destroying it or getting kicked out was by becoming mentally stable. Otherwise, we'd just be wasting our grant money. Yes, she was safe when she was in a hotel, but her behavior was so unpredictable, she would continue to get kicked out.

So, I told the team at the Center for Harm Reduction, and at the Refresh Spot to tell Patty my deal if they saw her. I would put her in another hotel if she agreed to take the shot. A couple of weeks later, I was driving with our outreach team in Skid Row after stopping by CHR to pick up some supplies. As we turned on to Towne Ave from Fourth Street, I saw a short, skinny woman pushing a cart full of precious cargo.

"Slow down, that's Patty!" I said.

The driver rolled down the window.

"Hey, Patty!"

"Oh, hi, Dr. Partovi."

I looked her in the eye. "I'll get you into a hotel when you take the shot."

Without hesitation or resistance, she said. "Okay, Dr. Partovi."

Hmmm. Would it be that easy?

The next day, Patty showed up at CHR, looking more clear-eyed and seeming more clear-headed. "I'm ready for my shot. I need to get off the streets."

"Do you understand this is the same medicine you were taking before?" I asked. "But this shot version lasts a month. This medicine will help keep your emotions stable," I said, using her wording. "This makes it easier, much easier than remembering to take your pills every day."

She said she understood. Somehow, she had come to terms with it and was perfectly fine accepting the shot. I gave it to her. That same day I texted Cesar's "brother," Peter, who owned the hotel where she had destroyed her room. "Can I put Patty in your hotel downtown? I just gave her a shot that will keep her calm and I promise she will behave." I anxiously watched the "reply" dots taunting me on the phone.

Finally, his answer: "Yes."

I couldn't believe he was giving her/us another chance. I called the person in charge of the grant so we could pay for her hotel stay. We piled her things into my car, went to the corner market for some bread, peanut butter, cigarettes, etc., to hold her over the weekend.

I texted my psychiatrist friend, "She took the shot!" She replied, "Congrats! But also, it's a little weird that you get so excited about giving shots!" I called her caseworker from FSP to arrange an interview, so they could help her get housing. And I called the person in charge of our outpatient drug treatment program about starting the process to get Patty into the program. She didn't have a phone, but Peter would send messages letting her know about appointments.

Over the next few days, Patty slept a lot. I'd check in with Peter, who'd tell me she was behaving and very pleasant.

Thank God!! I'd whisper each time.

The week that Patty's shot was due, I told everyone—those at CHR, the Refresh Spot, and Peter—to remind her to come in on Thursday. I was nervous she wouldn't come, but she did.

She asked about the shot. "That dose kind of dulled me," she said. "Can I get a lower dose?"

I texted my psychiatrist friend for advice on what dosage I should give and then gave her the lower dose.

I received an email from Maggie saying that Patty's funding through the grant was going to run out in two weeks. The grant money only pays for one month, per person. I told the FSP worker when she would need to have another option. They were able to find a place in South L.A. Patty needed a Covid-19 test to stay there, so I asked our nurse practitioner to swing by the hotel to administer one. While we waited the two days for the result, they placed her in quarantine, but by then, it was too late. She had taken off. The next day, she came to the clinic with a cart (never a good sign).

"I don't want to stay there," she told me. "They wouldn't let me out. They wouldn't let me smoke. I felt like I was in jail, and I've worked very hard to stay out of jail. I don't like being treated like that. And I would have to share a room. It's not safe! I used to gang bang in that area."

I was firm with her. "You have no other choice. We don't have any more funds for a hotel."

"I don't mean any disrespect, Dr. Partovi. I do appreciate all that you've done for me, but what about The Russ? Call them."

She was talking about a temporary housing facility in Skid Row. "It doesn't work that way." We went back-and-forth with more of the same. I was getting frustrated. "Patty," I said, "we worked hard to get you into this place. Please, just go. Put up with "feeling like you are in jail" for a little while. Your choice is this place or the streets."

Now stabilized and exhibiting reason, she chose the streets.

I'm not sure exactly what the issue really was, but there is something to be said about treating vulnerable people with respect and acceptance. This is a basic need we all have.

A couple of weeks later, she showed up for her shot. "Dr. Partovi, I want you to know that I've been looking around for a place. I need a letter from you and then I'll go to DMH. They're going to help." She was proud of herself for taking matters into her own hands, and so was I. She requested an even lower dose than the previous one, and I complied. She also agreed to the flu shot and another Covid-19 test. It was like Christmas.

The next week, one of our workers put her into a hotel that was a quarantine site for PEH who had been exposed to Covid-19 or were having symptoms.

She called me from the new hotel, and she was upbeat, even giggly. "I'm watching a lot of TV," she told me. "And get this Dr. Partovi, they give us shots of vodka! I'm getting into The Coronado (another interim housing site) next Monday!"

Talk about meeting people where they are! The county finally figured out that people who needed to stay in quarantine might also need to get high. They gave out marijuana, too. That's how we keep people safe!

The following week, Patty came into the clinic. "I'm at the Coronado!" she told us. "My daughter came over and did my hair! I'm right around the corner from Homeless Health Care and I'm in ITP (our outpatient drug treatment program). I go there on Monday, Wednesday, and Friday. And, if you're gonna be on vacation in two weeks," she added, "I should get my shot next week!"

Marinated.

24

I KNOW DEATH; HOPE FOR HAITI

I KNOW DEATH. I'M A DOCTOR. I'VE HAD PATIENTS DIE AFTER just meeting them, and I've had patients I've known for years die. You would think in my profession, I'd be accustomed to death. Old hat, run-of-the-mill death. On the contrary, throughout my career and personal life, death has been a haunting experience. With each encounter, I vow: *This will be my last.*

When one hears the word *death*, he or she might envision a loved one who has passed. But what do Americans think when they hear "air strike," "military action," or "a surge?" They may think about the protection of freedoms, or good vs. bad players, or that war is a "necessary evil." But I think of death. And it takes me back, always, to those haunting losses of patients or family members.

When a patient dies, there is suffering, immense grief, screams, yells, tears, and sometimes—nothing. Mary died of uterine cancer. I still remember her in the hospital, lying on her side. Her sisters told me she had something to discuss with me. She wanted to know what was going to happen and if she would be in pain. I knew how she would die; it wouldn't be peaceful, and she would suffer. Yet, her family would suffer the most. I didn't tell Mary that, but that's what I knew of death.

Robert and Paris died after heart failure; Vladimir, Ernesto, and Anne died as a result of overdoses; Pedro had terminal stomach cancer and Marlene leukemia; Nickenson died from complications of AIDS; my sister's partner, Sue, died in a car accident; an important mentor and my father both died of lung cancer; my half-brother suffered a sudden heart attack and died at age 62, Michelle finally passed at age 59, and my mother died in November, 2021, after suffering with Alzheimer's for many years.

When my father died, my entire family was decimated. My dad was the eldest of six, outlived by his parents. Watching his siblings and wife, and my grandparents grapple with their loss was suffering on a whole other level. Especially my grandparents. Watching them lose their son was practically unbearable. No one should have to experience their child's death.

In 2006, I started the Health Care Advocacy Group for UCLA's medical students. I had taken fourth-year students to Jamaica with Dr. Bruno Lewis as part of International Medicine Rotation for several years. But I realized I wanted to take third-year students, to have an earlier impact on their career decision-making. The students I knew were extremely passionate about healthcare for the underserved, and I wanted to take advantage of that passion and further cultivate realistic careers in poverty medicine. What we began to create back then has grown into a nonprofit corporation.

In December of 2009, four students and I went to Haiti. I had been to South Africa and India, but nothing prepared me for the utter despair of sick, malnourished children. Ten days after our return, Haiti was devastated by the earthquake of January 2010. Feeling called to go back and help, three weeks later I went to Port-Au-Prince, where I met Gladys Thomas, the director of The United States for the Children of Haiti. She was trying to direct the post-earthquake chaos at Hope Hospital. I stayed for two weeks, providing much-needed primary care and building lasting relationships with Gladys, Dr. Gousse, and my unofficially adopted son, Joel, who showed up to translate for us one day. Our nonprofit, Health, Empowerment, Advocacy and Learning (H.E.A.L.) provided scholarship money for Joel to attend medical school in the Dominican Republic.

I returned to Haiti every year, until the beginning of the Covid-19 pandemic. HEAL has taken many medical students to Haiti annually since 2009. Focused on the town of Mussote, we see an average of two to three hundred patients per day and provide primary care and medications to local schools and orphanages.

During my time in Haiti, I have experienced many children dying. It's difficult to explain what it's like to watch a child die. It's unnatural and wrong. These children died of malnutrition because of poverty. One could say that poverty is the result of racism, greed, and corruption. However, a child dying is a child dying.

Let's cease this suffering. I know death. Each one involves suffering and affects loved ones and communities. Look at your own child. Imagine how you would feel if they suffered. Children dying is not okay.

Following is an excerpt from my forthcoming memoir, *This is Haiti*, which details my experiences providing medical support to this vulnerable community. For further information about how you can get involved to affect change, please visit www.weareheal.com.

EXCERPT FROM *THIS IS HAITI*

Haiti: One Day at the Hospital,
Three Weeks After the Earthquake

WHEN I WALK INTO HOPE HOSPITAL, I SEE A REGULAR, A MAN with a foot abscess, waiting diligently for me.

"There aren't too many patients," announces Dr. Gousse, the medical director and my new BFF after spending my first week in Haiti. It's 2010, mere weeks after the devastating earthquake.

I change the dressing on the patient's foot, then go to check in with my AIDS patient with pneumonia. Joel, my translator, and Carolyn, one of the nurses, show up.

"Dr. Susan, there's an unconscious man outside," Carolyn says.

I point to a cot in the front section of the hospital. "Bring him here."

Shortly, four young men carry in another young man. He's large, and they strain to get him onto the cot. I hear someone say "asthma."

"Does he have asthma?" I ask.

Joel immediately translates for me and then says, "Yes."

The patient, Jonelle, had gone to work the day before, returned to his tent to sleep and was found unconscious this morning.

"Jonelle, wake up!" I rub his sternum with my knuckles. He is unresponsive to pain. I listen to his lungs. He is taking short, shallow breaths, barely moving any air through his lungs, and he sounds extremely wheezy.

"Kelly," I say, looking at one of the American volunteer nurses. "Go get the pulse-ox machine, nebulizer, and box of inhalation medications. All of it's in the 'ICU' because we're using it for the baby." We'd been treating a baby with breathing issues who was now stable.

She brings everything but the medication, saying she couldn't find the box. The plug for the equipment doesn't work and the cot is too low on the ground. I can't resuscitate someone on my knees.

I switch tactics. "Come on, guys. Let's move him to the ICU!" The four men pick up the heavy cot and dutifully follow me to the ICU. I run to the pharmacy downstairs. Organizing this small room had become my special project, and I had recently put all the emergency medications in one section. Grabbing the epinephrine and a special stash of Albuterol, I rush upstairs to meet everyone.

Shortly, Brian the pediatrician joins us. Jonelle's pulse-ox is in the seventies (normal is over ninety-five), but we have no ventilator available (there's only one in all of Port-au-Prince and it's at the new, private hospital).

"Want me to put in an IV?" Kelly asks, already gathering materials.

"Yes!" I give Jonelle an intramuscular shot of 1cc of epinephrine and get the nebulizer going.

"Did you check his eyes?" Kelly asks calmly, her voice piercing through the surrounding chaos.

Brian quickly checks Jonelle's eyes, and they're responsive.

"Okay, let's think," Brian says. "Why is he unresponsive?" He runs through the algorithm on how to evaluate and treat an unresponsive adult. I don't do this often, being a family physician. But Brian is closer to residency and spends more time with severely ill patients. He closes his eyes, takes a deep breath, then opens them again. "He doesn't seem to have overdosed on anything. Sugar. Check his sugar."

Kelly knows the ICU room well and quickly locates the glucometer, which only has two strips left. "It's twenty," she announces.

This is dangerously low. I hurry back to the emergency shelf in the pharmacy, remembering the two ampules of Dextrose there. As I reenter the ICU, one of the German nurses enters with an inquiring look on her face. After the earthquake, a German surgical group called Humedica set up shop at Hope Hospital; this brought doctors, nurses, medications and supplies to treat the many trauma patients resulting from the disaster.

"Are any anesthesiologists here?" I ask.

She rushes out and soon, two German anesthesiologists come rushing in. I gave them a quick version of the story.

"Push the sugar," says one of the anesthesiologists, handing me an airway. This means he wants to administer glucose through the IV, as much as possible. The airway is a contraption that holds an unconscious patient's tongue down so their breathing won't be impeded.

I give the airway to Brian because I don't know how to put it in, but he can't do it either. The anesthesiologist moves to the head of the cot and inserts a nasal trumpet, a big tube in the nose used to keep the tongue from blocking a patient's airway.

I'm so glad the anesthesiologists are here!

Jonelle starts to wake up. "Push more sugar," the taller one commands. Both are square-shouldered, with brown hair.

Kelly complies. We add Decadron to the IV list.

"Let's sit him up," I say, noticing that Jonelle is starting to fight with us. I turn the crank at the end of the bed, propping him into a sitting position. One anesthesiologist removes the nose trumpet and suddenly, Jonelle starts screaming. His eyes are wild.

Too much epi?

Jonelle is talking, but when I look at Joel for translation, he tells us the patient is speaking nonsense.

We continue to stand around him, trying to offer him the nebulizer and oxygen, but he refuses.

Joel listens then tells us that Jonelle says his right shoulder hurts. The patient keeps turning from one side to the other, trying to get comfortable, all while refusing his nebulizer and oxygen. His pulse ox is now more stable, in the eighties. He's awake, and I'm satisfied. We decide to give him room to calm down.

When we return later in the day to check on Jonelle, his pulse-ox is ninety-two and his heart rate is a hundred. He's sleeping on his tummy, finally comfortable. He does have a fever, so I add antibiotics to his regimen.

Joel and I head downstairs to see Jean. I administer Azithromycin and a final shot of Ceftriaxone for his pneumonia. I tell him he can go home the following day. We advise him to follow up at GHESKIO's satellite AIDS clinic at Community Hospital. During his admission, we diagnosed him with HIV. Jean reminds me to give him a referral.

Later that evening, family members are singing somewhere in the hospital. It sounds like they've created their own church service. Suddenly, a family member of one of the inpatients comes to me and says a little girl isn't breathing normally. I take a couple of steps toward this young girl, who is lying on her side and looks about four years old. I ask where her family members are. A few people begin to gather, shaking their heads—which, I guess means no one is there with her.

She's drooling and blood trickles from her nose. I look under her clothes, doing a brief exam, and notice blood in her diapers. Gently, I turn her onto her back. "Tell me what's going on, little girl," I say. Her eyes are open, but she's unresponsive.

I find a card that serves as her "chart." I learn that Brian admitted her earlier in the day with gastroenteritis (diarrhea) and possible bronchitis. I see an empty bowl nearby. She has finished her rice and beans, which is a good sign. I listen to her heart and hear congestion in her lungs. I tell Joel to go upstairs and bring the pulse-ox and breathing machine down, because we only have one of each.

"Take it off the asthma guy?" he asks.

"Yes," I say. "He's doing fine." As I turn my attention back to the girl, her eyes start twitching to the left. *Oh, shit, I've seen this before. The little girl in the rural town of Cazale who died of complications from malnutrition.*

I put my new patient back onto her side and ask a nurse to retrieve injectable diazepam (used to stop seizures), another medication I found and put on my emergency shelf. The girl's body feels hot, so I instruct another nurse to get some rectal Tylenol.

The eye twitching is probably a febrile seizure, a tremor that can occur in children who have a high fever. The pulse ox tells me her oxygen level is 100 percent. *Okay, she's out of it because she was seizing.*

One minute after giving her the diazepam, she stops seizing. Right then, Kelly and one of the Germans, Simone, return from an excursion to the beach. Their smiles fade immediately when they see what I'm doing.

They jump into action. "What do you need?"

"Normal saline," I say. This is for hydration. I also decide to call Brian.

I quickly fill him in on the situation, and he offers to come to the hospital. Simone sends the driver to fetch him.

When I check again, the girl's oxygen level has dropped to the seventies. I try to reposition her head to make sure her airway is open, and I give her a breathing treatment with a nebulizer.

Simone is an EMT, and he comes back with bag-valve-mask at the same moment Brian shows up. He starts to apply the bag, holding the mask over the girl's face. As he does so, he tells me what he knows about her case.

"She was supposed to go home today," he says. "Her mom said she was feeling better."

"She's bleeding a lot from her rectum and her belly looks distended," I say.

He listens to her belly. "She has bowel sounds. Ruptured appendix?"

"That would be my guess in the states. Here, I would say typhoid and a perforated bowel."

"But she didn't have a fever earlier," Brian says.

I head to the pharmacy and grab all the antibiotics I can find: ceftriaxone, gentamycin, and clindamycin.

Gladys, the director of the hospital, calls Germaine, the hospital keeper. I tell her about the young girl, hoping to learn where we can transfer her. Gladys's phone keeps going out, but I finally get an answer: "Community Hospital."

Brian, Simone, and I struggle with the adult-sized bag. Simone calls over to the camp, where the Germans are staying, and asks someone to bring over pediatric resuscitating tools.

Brian decides to insert a nasogastric tube in her nose, hoping to decompress the girl's belly. Kelly finds some kind of tube, and the little girl groans as he places it. I like the groan—it means she's responsive. As Brian aspirates her belly, suddenly blood begins to pour out of the NG tube.

"What the hell is going on? DIC?" He shakes his head. Disseminated intravascular coagulation. This is when someone's clotting abilities are out of whack, causing spontaneous bleeding and/or blood clots. Usually, it's caused by a severe infection that has spread to the bloodstream. It's a bad sign, and often leads to death.

One of the German anesthesiologists arrives bearing a large bag of supplies. He pulls out a pediatric bag, which is used to squeeze air into the lungs—like mouth-to-mouth, only using a bag and mask. Soon, the girl's pulse-ox goes up.

The girl's father arrives, and Joel tells him what's going on. He asks if it is okay that we take her to the hospital. Luckily, the father is on board with our decisions.

When I return from speaking with the father, the girl is lying on her side. Her pulse ox is at 100 percent. Maybe she has a pneumothorax (a punctured lung that might worsen or improve with position changes).

But the danger returns quickly. I turn briefly to speak to a nurse and when I turn back around, I see Brian doing chest compressions. The scene proceeds as if in slow motion. My heart clenches.

"She stopped breathing?" I ask.

"Her heart stopped beating," Brian answers, in between counts. I tell Joel to get the girl's father. *Brian is pushing hard on her chest.*

"What's the epi dose?" Brian asks in a calm voice tinged with desperation.

I pull out my miniature, advanced life-saving book. It's amazing how sometimes everything you learn goes out the window in times of crisis. Thank goodness for cheat sheets.

"Let's go over the possible causes of pulseless-ness." I read from my book: "Hypoxia" (low oxygen). *Well, yeah.* "Hypoglycemia" (low sugar). *But we already gave her dextrose.* "Hypo/hyperkalemia." *Her potassium levels, but the lab's closed so there's no way to tell if that's the cause.* "Acidosis" (the bloodstream becomes too acidic). *Possibly.* "Tamponade" (the heart lining is filled with blood, impeding the heart's ability to pump).

"It could be a pneumothorax or hemothorax," I say. This is a collapsed lung or blood in the lung. "Her oxygen level improved when she was on her left side, so it would be on the left side."

At this, Brian grabs a needle. The anesthesiologist takes over administering chest compressions.

Brian squats down next to the little girl. "One, two, three, one, two, three," the anesthesiologist counts out. Brian goes in on three. Blood starts pouring out. I grab a syringe and attach it to the needle, and 10cc of blood is drawn. Brian looks around for a place to empty the syringe, so I quickly grab her rice and beans bowl, and he squirts the blood inside. I reattach the needle to the syringe, and he fills it again.

It's a lot of blood. "Did you hit the heart?" I ask, alarmed.

"No, I don't think so," he says. But he sounds unsure.

As the blood flow slows a little, we decide it's not the heart.

"How long since the first epi?" I ask.

"Five and a half minutes," Simone says.

"Check a pulse," I order. Nothing. They give her another epi, and I grab an atropine, another medicine to get the heart pumping.

Brian nods. "Sure, give it a try."

We are bagging, pushing, bagging, pushing. I look down at the braids in her hair. *This is why I didn't go into pediatrics. I don't want to deal with dying children. Do ER docs look at the braids in kids' hair?*

"How long has it been?" I ask.

"Twenty-five minutes."

"Look for a pulse."

We all give it a try. Nothing. One of the onlookers asks in broken English, "Doctor Susan, dead?"

I nod. "Joel, get the dad."

A moment later, he enters the room.

"I'm so sorry," I say, and Joel translates. "She didn't make it. I'm so sorry. She died." I want to be clear.

He shakes his head with tears in his eyes. That's when I begin to tear up. I glance behind me. Big, burly Simone is crying. The anesthesiologist is shaking his head.

Brian's shirt is soaked with sweat. "This has never happened to me," he says in disbelief. "I don't know what happened to her. I didn't learn anything."

When I decided to return to Haiti, one of my friends asked if I was prepared for the tragic emotional upheaval the earthquake had caused. I told her I had already experienced Haiti's tragic emotional upheaval when I had visited the previous December. Don't get me wrong—seeing hundreds of buildings crumbled to millions of tiny blocks and knowing people were dead among the rubble was tragic. Hearing so many stories about firsthand experiences during the earthquake was completely heart-wrenching. The numerous tent cities erected after the earthquake were overwhelming, women lining up for blocks waiting for rice or water distribution was troubling.

But these weren't the only emotions I experienced while I was there two weeks after the earthquake. Mostly, I saw people getting back to work, selling their goods on the sidewalk, and singing in the evenings. At the clinic, family members stayed with their post-op relatives, telling them stories to make them laugh and smiling whenever I passed by. "Dokte Susan," they called me. I met smiling kids who asked me to take their pictures so they could see themselves in my camera. On the streets, people smiled and waved as I passed by.

In December before the earthquake, I had ventured to work in Cazale, at a rural clinic, with four medical students. This was my first trip to Haiti. I had been excited to work in a rural, underdeveloped country—something I had dreamt of since working in Mexico and deciding to pursue a career in medicine. I was working with a small group of UCLA medical students, teaching them about advocacy for those with little access to healthcare. This was before Obamacare. In Haiti, I would work at a nurse-run medical clinic. By then, my students were in their third year, just starting to experience evaluating real patients. We planned the trip for months. We fundraised, purchased medications, and tried to learn Creole. The clinic was run by an American missionary nurse married to a Haitian man. Next door was a malnutrition center, run by her sister, also a missionary and married to a Haitian. The malnutrition center would accept children from the surrounding, mountainous villages.

When we arrived, around sixty miniature bodies with big bellies and good appetites swarmed around the center. On arrival, the nurses put IVs into the veins in their scalps (the easiest method when a kid is so dehydrated) and they would care for them until they were well enough to go over to the center, steps away. The children ate peanut butter around the clock after tolerating days of oral rehydration. It was miraculous to watch. However, these were extremely sick, fragile kids. One problem could cause a rapid spiral to death. If they started to vomit or experienced diarrhea or any other usually benign illness, they would end up back at the clinic, where there was, basically, a pediatric ICU. By then, the young patients usually died. The students and I experienced child after child dying. I was expected to treat these dying children with no laboratory capability, no ability to intubate or give blood. I was not a pediatrician nor an emergency physician, and the experience stretched me beyond my limits. I remember each kid that died.

Two weeks after the earthquake, I hadn't experienced this hopeless gravity again—until this night. When Brian said, "I didn't learn anything," I knew what he meant. There was no explanation for the little girl's death. But I remembered my experience in Cazale and all the unexplained tragedies there. I thought—this is Haiti.

The young girl died after the earthquake, but she would have died before the earthquake, too. The father admitted to Joel that she had been sick for a month. Someone else told him later that the parents couldn't afford to bring her food while she was in the hospital. Germaine, the hospital keeper, had brought her the rice and beans.

Children dying senseless deaths due to poverty—that was my experience in Haiti. The earthquake's rubble will slowly get cleaned up and the surgery wounds will heal, but the Haiti I know will always exist until all of Haiti's children are well-fed and vaccinated, until they have access to clean drinking water, proper sanitation, education and medical care, and until all of Haiti's parents can remain healthy enough to live with and care for their children.

Over the next ten years, I continued to take medical students and attending physicians to Haiti. My best friend from medical school started coming with me; eventually, we founded HEAL, a nonprofit organization that works to continue our efforts to bring health care and education to Haitian practitioners and anyone wanting to work with this population.

I strive to work with the most vulnerable members of our society and guide learners to do the same. Haitians have suffered discrimination for centuries and as a result, are incredibly impoverished. They have endured decades of needless death and corruption. People experiencing homelessness, especially those suffering with severe mental illness and addiction, also are discriminated against. Left to fester in the streets or rotate in and out of jail or the hospital, they return to the streets again and again. The world and our society need to see one another as a "we." We are all the same. We all struggle with demons, and we all desire a joyful world for ourselves and family. I've been blessed with living in a country that has educated me and given me opportunities, provides security and allows me to vote. If I have an emergency, I can call 911. In my city, roads are repaired so I can easily travel. We have a functional justice system. Haitians, people experiencing homelessness, the mentally ill, and those suffering with addictions don't always have access to these blessings. I choose to take a stand to provide them with medical care and kindness so they can thrive, connect with loved ones, contribute to society and have purpose in their lives. Join me.